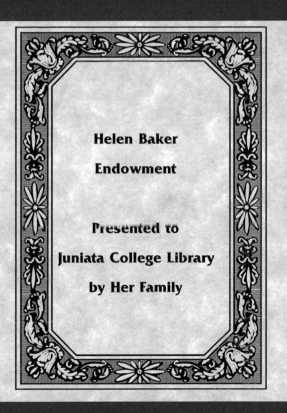

THE

BIRTH

THEY CALLED THEMSELVES THE K.K.K.

OF AN

AMERICAN

TERRORIST GROUP

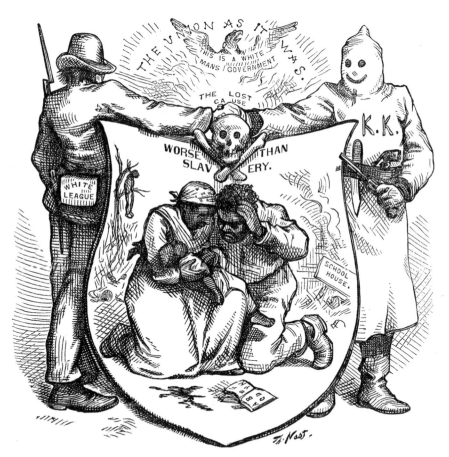

BY SUSAN CAMPBELL BARTOLETTI

Houghton Mifflin
Houghton Mifflin Harcourt
Boston New York

"The method of force which hides itself in secrecy is a method as old as humanity. The kind of thing that men are afraid or ashamed to do openly, and by day, they accomplish secretly, masked, and at night. The method has certain advantages. It uses Fear to cast out Fear; it dares things at which open method hesitates; it may with a certain impunity attack the high and the low; it need hesitate at no outrage of maiming or murder; it shields itself in the mob mind and then throws over all a veil of darkness which becomes glamor. It attracts people who otherwise could not be reached. It harnesses the mob."

—*W. E. B. Du Bois, 1935*

Houghton Mifflin is an imprint of Houghton Mifflin Harcourt Publishing Company.

www.hmhbooks.com

Book design by YAY! Design
The text of this book is set in Adobe Garamond Pro.

Library of Congress Cataloging-in-Publication Data

Bartoletti, Susan Campbell.
  They called themselves the K.K.K. : the birth of an American terrorist group / by Susan Campbell Bartoletti.
    p. cm.
  ISBN 978-0-618-44033-7
  1. Ku Klux Klan (19th cent.)—Juvenile literature.
  2. Ku Klux Klan (1915–)—Juvenile literature. 3. Racism—United States—History—Juvenile literature. 4. Hate groups—United States—History Juvenile literature. 5. United States—Race relations.
  I. Title.
    HS2330.K63B37 2010
    322.4'20973— dc22

                    2009045247

Manufactured in China
LEO 10 9 8 7 6 5 4 3 2
4500272473

Title page photo credit: *Harper's Weekly,* October 24, 1874; Library of Congress

Contents page photo credit: Albion Tourgée, *A Fool's Errand, by One of the Fools: The Famous Romance of American History* (New York: Fords, Howard, & Hulbert, 1879)

Contents

A NOTE TO THE READER

In the pages of this book, you will meet people who lived during the years that followed the Civil War, a time known as Reconstruction. These people come from a variety of backgrounds. You will read the stories of the Ku Klux Klansmen and their victims from a variety of sources, including congressional testimony, interviews, and historical journals, diaries, and newspapers.

Wherever possible, I have let the people of the past speak in their own voices. Some of these people use crude language. No matter how difficult it is to see the offensive words in print, I have made no attempt to censor these historical statements.

You will see images from pictorial newspapers such as *Harper's Weekly* and *Frank Leslie's Illustrated Newspaper* and other sources. These images depict people, events, and viewpoints of the time. Some of the depictions are caricatured and are racially offensive. I deeply regret any offense or hurt caused by the images, but again I have chosen not to censor.

You will also meet former slaves who were interviewed more than seventy years after the end of the Civil War. These interviews are commonly referred to as the Slave Narratives. Most of these men and women were children or young adults in their teens and early twenties when the Civil War ended, and were in their eighties and nineties when interviewed by government reporters in the late 1930s.

The government reporters— mostly white men and women— were instructed to transcribe or write the words in a way that reflected the interviewees' speech patterns. As a result, some of the dialect may be difficult to read. Even so, I have chosen not to alter the interviews or transpose the dialect into standardized English.

CHAPTER 1

"Bottom Rail Top"

I n the spring of 1865, as rain softened the hard ground, plenty of work was found for every pair of hands on the Williams plantation in Camden, Arkansas, despite the Civil War, which was still raging at the end of its fourth year.

Field hands chopped away old withered cotton stalks to make room for this year's seeds. Plow hands hitched mules to plows and furrowed the fields, turning over mile after mile of rich black dirt. Other slaves followed the plow, sowing the seeds and working manure into the furrows and building up the cotton beds.

Near the Big House, slave children worked in groups, too, stooping over vegetable garden rows, pulling weeds, plucking insects from the green shoots, harvesting the early vegetables, and readying the damp earth for the warm-season seeds.

Inside the Big House, there was plenty of work, too. For fourteen-year-old Mittie Williams, who

In this illustration, called *The Rising Generation*, children climb fence rails that represent the upper, middle, and bottom economic classes of Southern society.

Albion Winegar Tourgée, *The Invisible Empire*

A war artist for *Frank Leslie's Illustrated Newspaper* depicts invading Yankee soldiers plundering a Southern farm as they forage for food.

Library of Congress

worked as a house slave, there was Miss Eliza to tend to. Ever since Old Master died—in the South, use of the word *old* indicated respect for the person's years—Mittie had become the elderly woman's constant companion. "She skeered to stay by herself," Mittie recalled seventy-two years later.

Miss Eliza had reason to be afraid. Like most white Southerners, she would have known that the Confederacy was disintegrating and that Yankees were sweeping over the South. Frightening tales traveled from plantation to plantation, telling how Yankee soldiers were ransacking houses, turning the air thick with feathers as they ripped open mattresses and beds, searching for guns and silver and other valuables. How the Yankees swarmed over fields, stealing horses and hogs and chickens and molasses and flour, leaving little to eat. How the roads were littered with wasted carcasses of hogs and cattle. To Miss Eliza and other white Southerners, the Yankees were blue devils, determined to destroy the South, to starve out the Rebels and ruin their property, leaving them broken and destitute.

House slaves such as Mittie often overheard their masters and other white people holding political conversations and discussing the progress of the Civil War. Whatever news the slaves picked up about the "Freedom War," as they called it, they were quick to pass on to others along the "grapevine telegraph." The grapevine telegraph carried news, gossip, and rumors as it wound its way informally from person to person, plantation to plantation.

Some rumors were true. It was through the grapevine telegraph that many slaves had learned about the Emancipation Proclamation, which President Abraham Lincoln had signed two years earlier, on January 1, 1863. The Emancipation Proclamation decreed that all slaves in the eleven Rebel states and their territories were free. Two years later, in January 1865, as Northern victory became inevitable, Congress passed the Thirteenth Amendment, a law that abolished slavery *everywhere* in the United States and granted Congress the power to enforce the amendment. (It would take nearly a year for Congress to ratify, or formally adopt the Thirteenth Amendment.)

And enforce the amendment the Union army did. Mittie might have heard how the Yankees marched throughout the South, acting as an army of liberation, telling the slaves they were free—as free as any white person. Although many white Northerners did not favor racial equality, most supported emancipation, because as one Union soldier from Illinois wrote his parents, "Slavery stands in the way of putting down the rebellion." By freeing the slaves and ruining plantations, the Yankees were waging total war, destroying the South's agricultural economy and bringing the Rebels to their knees on the home front.

In the last days of fighting, Confederate leaders warned white

"I never, in my life, felt more certain that I was doing right, than I do in signing this paper," said Lincoln about the Emancipation Proclamation. "If my name ever goes into history it will be for this act, and my whole soul is in it." The Proclamation did not free the slaves in the border states that sided with the Union.

Library of Congress

With great emotion, black Union soldiers liberate slaves on a North Carolina plantation.

Harper's Weekly, January 23, 1864; Library of Congress

Southerners that if the South lost the war, the slaves would rule over their former masters and other whites. This false rumor was scare talk, intended to whip white Southerners into a state of great fear and make them hate the Yankees even more, but many white Southerners believed it could happen.

Some rumors were half-truths, as when the slaves heard that the federal government intended to give black families forty acres carved out of their former master's land, as well as a mule, just as soon as the North won the war. "We heard that lots of slaves was getting land and some mules to set up for theirselves," recalled Mittie.

In reality, the government had passed a special order that would have permitted some slave families to rent confiscated land, parcels up to forty acres in size for three years, with the possibility to buy. As the news traveled, slave men and women grew excited about the crops they'd raise to eat and to sell and the homes they'd build once they had their land. But the allocation of land had hardly begun before the federal government revoked the special order.

Despite her fear of the Yankees, Miss Eliza granted Mittie and her father permission to go fishing one Sunday in April. No sooner had Mittie cast her line into the river than cannons began to boom in the distance.

Right away, Mittie's father knew what the thundering cannons meant. "Pappy jumps up, throws down his pole and everything, and grabs my hand and starts flying towards the house," recalled Mittie. " 'It's victory,' he keep on saying. 'It's freedom. Now we'se gwine be free.' "

Victory came on April 9, 1865, the day that the Confederate general Robert E. Lee surrendered his army to Ulysses S. Grant, commander of the Union army, at Appomattox Court House, a village in Virginia. As news of Lee's surrender spread through the Union army camps, wild jubilation broke out among Yankee soldiers.

On April 9, 1865, the Confederate general Robert E. Lee (right) surrenders to the Union general Ulysses S. Grant (left).

Currier and Ives, Library of Congress

Cannons all over boomed, signaling the fall of the Confederacy. Within a few weeks, the remaining Confederate generals all surrendered.

The war that had seemed endless was over, and with it, two hundred and fifty years of bondage for black Americans were also over.

Slavery had mocked the ideals of a nation

dedicated to freedom and equality. Now as the United States faced Reconstruction, or the work of putting the country back together, it had the chance to live up to its creed.

It wouldn't be easy. Racism was deeply embedded in white society in the North as well as the South. It would take many years for white Americans to understand what freedom meant for black Americans. For two hundred and fifty years, white people had occupied the top rails in society, and black people, the bottom rail.

It would be especially difficult in the South, where most black people lived. There, they were understood only as an inferior race, as property that could be bought and sold and exploited in order to produce wealth for white people.

Most white Southerners believed that God created black people for the special purpose of working and serving white people. To them, the thought of racial equality was immoral because it violated God's plan. "Such equality does not in fact exist and never can," explained a Georgia state supreme court judge in 1869. "The God of nature made it otherwise. . . . From the tallest archangel in heaven to the meanest reptile on earth, moral and social inequities exist, and must continue to exist throughout all eternity."

Even after the Confederacy's surrender, many white Southerners felt certain that black people still had to belong to someone. "If they don't belong to me, whose are they?" asked one white woman from Virginia about her former slaves.

"'Course she is our nigger," said a Missouri woman to her husband about their seventeen-year-old house slave. "She is as much our nigger now as she was the day you bought her two years ago and paid fifteen hundred dollars for her."

Most white Southern families did not own slaves. Those who did—about one out of every four families—felt anger at the loss of their valuable human property. Before the war, each slave was worth about one thousand dollars, or thirteen thousand dollars today. The average slaveholder owned between one and nine slaves, and some of the wealthiest planters owned hundreds.

Many slaveholders expected the federal government to compensate them for their great monetary loss.

The wife of an Alabama planter bitterly described her family's situation. "We had all our earnings swept away," wrote Victoria Clayton. "The Government of the United States has the credit of giving the black man his freedom, while it was at the expense of the Southern people."

A Mississippi planter described the devastation that he and other planters suffered in addition to the loss of their slaves. "We came out of the war utterly broken up," said Samuel Gholson, a former Confederate brigadier general and slaveholder. "We lost all our stock; the slaves were emancipated; on a great many plantations houses and fencing were burned; and we were out of provisions, and at least ninety-nine men out of a hundred in debt; having nothing left but our land."

White Southerners such as Victoria Clayton and Samuel Gholson did not consider the financial losses suffered by generations of slave families. All told, some modern historians estimate that slaves lost a total $3.4 billion worth of unpaid labor, or more than $17 billion today. Other scholars estimate the loss as much higher, possibly $1.4 trillion or $4.7 trillion, respectively.

As Samuel Gholson points out, all many planters and farmers had left was their land, and as they regarded their fields, they

This 1865 photograph of ruined houses shows the total destruction that some planters suffered in Savannah, Georgia, possibly as a result of the Union bombardment or General Sherman's campaign, known as the "march to the sea."

Library of Congress

During the war the Confederacy printed paper money, as shown here. By the spring of 1864, it took forty-six dollars to buy an item that had cost one dollar at the start of the war in 1861. By the war's end, Confederate money was nearly worthless. Library of Congress

worried about their future and getting back on their feet financially. Slave labor had raised more than half of the tobacco crops, three-quarters of the cotton, and nearly all of the rice, sugar, and hemp. Now that the slaves were freed, who would cultivate and harvest the hundreds of thousands of acres, and how much would it cost? Most planters and farmers had no cash or sources of credit to pay wages. The war had made their Confederate money worthless. On top of these losses, the Confederate states owed $712 million in war debts.

White Southerners who had not owned slaves also worried about their future. Some of these people lived in towns and ran stores or businesses, but most were yeoman farmers or farmers who owned small plots of land. Before the war, these small farmers had aspired to own larger farms and to acquire slaves in order to produce more crops, which would in turn increase their wealth. Now these men would compete with the freed people over land and cash crops.

The lowest class of white Southerners consisted of poor, unskilled laborers who owned no land and worked for other white

In this caricatured engraving, Yankee soldiers liberate slaves at a planter's house. White Southerners feared that liberation would turn the social order upside down.

Harper's Weekly, April 4, 1863; Library of Congress

people. These whites feared that black people might take their jobs.

In the eyes of most white Southerners, emancipation threatened to turn their society upside down, with black people on top and white people on the bottom. They also feared that black people would get grand ideas, thinking that freedom made them as good as—or even better than—white people. Rumors spread about black people who flaunted their freedom and new station. Four months after surrender, *Harper's Weekly* reported a gleeful reaction from a black Union soldier who spotted his former master among a group of Confederate prisoners. "Hello, massa," he shouted. "Bottom rail top dis time."

The soldier's flagrant disregard for racial etiquette likely outraged his former master: in the South a black person was forbidden to speak to a white person unless spoken to first, let alone flaunt his freedom and his new station. To many white Southerners, this small violation of racial etiquette would have reinforced their greatest fear: the bottom rail *was* on top.

A former slave from Texas remembered the warning about wounded white pride that his father had given him near the war's end, when he was eighteen. "My father kept pointing out that the War wasn't going to last forever," recalled Martin Jackson, "but that our forever was going to be spent living among the Southerners, after they got licked."

President Abraham Lincoln called for a swift and lenient Reconstruction. "With malice toward none; with charity for all," President Lincoln had offered in his second inaugural address just a few weeks before Lee's surrender. "Let us strive . . . to bind up the nation's wounds [and to achieve] a just, and a lasting peace."

But Lincoln would not live to guide the country through Reconstruction and a just and lasting peace. Just five days after Lee's surrender, a Southern sympathizer gunned down the president.

Abraham Lincoln was shot on April 14, 1865, and died the next morning. That day, Vice President Andrew Johnson took the oath as president. Library of Congress

"I 'lect [recollect] Uncle Charlie Burns what drive de buggy for Massa Charles, come runnin' out in de yard and holler, 'Everybody free, everybody free,' and purty soon sojers comes and de captain reads a 'mation [proclamation]. And Law me, dat one time Massa Charley can't open he mouth, 'cause de captain tell him to shut up, dat he'd do de talkin'. Den de captain say, 'I come to tell you de slaves is free and you don't have to call nobody master no more.'"

—Sarah Ford. Ford was about fifteen the day the Yankees arrived on the Texas plantation. In 1936 she recalled that her master didn't like her father, because "he had spirit." Her spirited father immediately borrowed a wagon, loaded up his family, and moved to another part of Texas, where he built a cabin on a patch of land. Library of Congress

CHAPTER 2

"Boys, Let Us Get Up a Club"

I n the days and weeks that followed surrender, battle-weary
Confederate soldiers began to wind their way home across rut-
ted roads, fallow fields, and burned-out homes and barns. Most
were on foot, and they felt grateful for two things: they were alive,
and they had been permitted to keep their mules or horses, which
they desperately needed to plant a spring crop. Some had been permitted to keep their service revolvers and government-issued guns.

In Tennessee, six Confederate officers found their hometown of
Pulaski clouded with gloom and disappointment. Like most white
Southerners who had sided with the Confederacy, these men—John
Lester, Calvin Jones, Richard Reed, James Crowe, Frank McCord,
and John Kennedy—believed they had fought valiantly for a noble
cause: to preserve a government and way of life that they considered
superior and a covenant with God, only to be defeated by a more
powerful industrial North. The despair they felt at their "Lost Cause"
filled their letters and diaries. So did defiance and fear at what the
coming months might bring.

The Pulaski townspeople, like countless white Southerners,
felt a deep sense of grief and loss. Their beloved state had sent more
than 110,000 soldiers to the Confederates; 31,000 other Tennesseans
fought for the Union. Now hatred and strife festered like an open sore

**Four of the six Pulaski men are shown in these photographs taken about twenty years
after the war: (from top) John C. Lester, James R. Crowe, Calvin Jones, and John Kennedy.
Missing: Richard Reed and Frank McCord.** Tennessee State Library and Archives

In this illustration, the crosses symbolize the Confederacy's Lost Cause, a term coined by white Southerners after the war. The stars in the Rebel flag light the night sky.

Currier and Ives, 1872, Library of Congress

among relatives and friends who had chosen opposing sides.

All that fall and winter after surrender, town newspapers such as the *Pulaski Citizen* published lists of the Confederate dead. Bodies were still being recovered and identified, relatives notified.

Most white Southerners scarcely knew a family that didn't mourn a relative or friend killed or wounded in the war. Nearly one out of every five Confederate soldiers ages thirteen to forty-three were dead from battle wounds or from camp diseases such as typhoid, dysentery, and pneumonia. Throughout the countryside and on the city and town streets, black mourning wreaths and ribbons hung from doors; widows and mothers of fallen sons were garbed in black dresses; and veteran soldiers hobbled on crutches, some with empty trouser legs or empty shirtsleeves pinned in place.

Tennessee had witnessed more battles than any other state except Virginia, including three of the deadliest battles of the war. But it wasn't just the dead soldiers that the Pulaski citizens grieved; they also grieved the battle-scarred land, with its charred, limbless trees. Shattered hills. Burned-up houses. Ruined plantations. Miles of broken fences. Empty henhouses and hog pens. Artillery had caused much of the damage; marauding Yankees were to blame for the rest.

The Pulaski townspeople also felt pain and anger at the sight of the Union flag that flew over their courthouse. As in most Southern towns, Union soldiers swarmed everywhere, taking charge, flaunting their blue uniforms and victory. In newspaper editorials, the feelings of white Southern writers oscillated between anger and dread. To them, peace seemed almost as terrible to bear as war.

The returning six soldiers didn't admit in writing to these feelings. Instead, one of the men later described the days after the war as full of restlessness and boredom. He attributed the feelings to the return to civilian life and to the strict restrictions imposed on the men

A man sits in the scarred Tennessee countryside where Union soldiers carried Missionary Ridge in November 1863. The three-day battle left 5,815 Union men and 6,670 Confederates dead.

Library of Congress

who had fought for or otherwise supported the Confederacy.

"[We] could not engage at once in business or professional pursuits," explained John Lester, a captain in the Tennessee Confederate infantry. "Few had capital to enter mercantile or agricultural enterprises. There was a total lack of amusements and social diversions which prevail wherever society is in a normal condition."

To pass the time, the six friends got in the habit of meeting at night in a law office that belonged to Calvin Jones's father. There is no record of their conversations during these evenings. But as the men were well educated—most were college graduates and four aspired to be lawyers and one became editor of the *Pulaski Citizen*—it's likely that they discussed the politics of Reconstruction of the Union.

The painful subject of Reconstruction was on every white Southerner's mind. How would the United States be put back together? How would the North treat the eleven Confederate states and their war heroes? Who would head the local and state governments in the South? Would the North let the South choose its own leaders?

At night the men lounged in this Pulaski law office belonging to Judge M. Jones, father of Calvin Jones.

Tennessee State Library and Archives

Would the North allow the South to get on its feet again? Or would the North fix the rules to suit itself?

The men had reason to worry. Like most Confederates, they were Democrats, and the Republicans were in control now. Although some moderate Republicans believed that the South had suffered enough, radical Republicans wanted the defiant South to pay, and to pay bitterly. They blamed the South for the war—a war that cost nearly 620,000 lives on both sides and 1 million wounded. It was a frightful toll for a nation that totaled 31 million people, a number that compares to 5 million troops dead today. The war cost was staggering in economic terms, too, as direct costs exceeded an estimated $6.6 billion, or nearly $22 trillion today.

In 1864, Republicans nominated Andrew Johnson, a Democratic senator from Tennessee who remained loyal to the Union during the war. Republicans hoped the Southern-born Johnson would unite the country.

Library of Congress

The six Pulaski men may have discussed the new president's plan for the South. Abraham Lincoln had been a Republican, but his vice president, Andrew Johnson, was a Southern Democrat from Tennessee. Although Johnson had sided with the Union during the war, he sided with the South over Reconstruction. As a native-born Southerner, Johnson understood his fellow white Southerners, and he shared their views on politics and race. As a Democrat, Johnson believed in limited government.

After Lincoln's death, Johnson took the oath of office. He began to reconstruct the Southern states on his own, without the help of

Congress, which was not in session. Right away, he began to pardon former Confederate soldiers and other supporters of the Confederate army. All these men had to do was swear an oath of loyalty to the United States. Then they could become citizens again and exercise their right to vote.

Johnson did not immediately pardon the most important Confederates, about 10,000 to 15,000 men in all. Any white Southern man who was somebody during the war had to travel to Washington and request a special pardon from President Johnson in order to vote again. These individuals included former federal officials, high-ranking Confederate officers, political leaders, and graduates of West Point or Annapolis who had joined or aided the Confederacy, and all ex-Confederates whose taxable property was worth more than $20,000, or about $262,625 today.

These powerful men belonged to the planter class, the wealthy men who owned thousands of acres of land and, before the war, hundreds of slaves. It angered them that men who were nobodies before the war could vote but important men like themselves could not until they were officially pardoned.

Some prideful Confederates refused to swear allegiance to a government that was, in their eyes, deliberately humiliating them. Most, however, wanted to take the oath, to become citizens again, and the sooner the better, so they could vote. They didn't want outsiders telling them what to do, especially *carpetbaggers,* as they disparagingly called the Northern Republicans who moved south, carrying all their belongings in a carpetbag, or suitcase, and who seemed determined to take advantage of the defeated South.

It's possible that the six men from Pulaski discussed the issue of the freed people, too. What should be done with the four million freed men, women, and children who made up 40 percent of the South's total population? There was no doubt the former slaves were free, but free to do what?

In vast numbers, the freed people were leaving the plantations and farms to roam the countryside. Some were searching for family

In this half-finished sketch, Confederate soldiers in Richmond, Virginia, swear an oath of loyalty to the United States. While newsworthy events were photographed as early as the 1850s, newspapers could only publish engravings. Newspapers either sent sketch artists to render drawings that could become engravings or hired engravers to create engravings from photographs. Alfred Waud, Library of Congress

members sold in slavery to distant plantations. Others were looking for new places to live and to work. Some were moving to Southern cities and towns, crowding into shantytowns, looking for schools, food, and medical care. Some were trying to escape cruel masters or trying to get north.

As the former slaves exercised their new freedom, they created a labor shortage for the planters and farmers, who needed them to cultivate and harvest the crops. Desperate to control the labor, some

A freedman is sold to pay his fine in Monticello, Florida, as legislated by the Black Codes.

Frank Leslie's Illustrated Newspaper, January 19, 1867; Library of Congress

planters and farmers used force, even killing those freed slaves who dared to leave. They also turned to their state and local governments for help in coercing the freed men, women, and children back to work in the fields. Encouraged by President Johnson, Southern lawmakers quickly passed laws called the Black Codes.

Most of the Black Codes were based on the former Slave Codes. The laws varied from state to state and even from town to town, but

all severely restricted the lives of the freed people, just as the Slave Codes had. Once more, the freed people were forced to work in labor gangs from sunup to sundown. They were forbidden to have visitors, hold meetings, and leave plantations without permission.

Other aspects of the Black Codes were based on Northern vagrancy laws. Unemployed black people were arrested and fined for vagrancy. If unable to pay their fines, they were auctioned off to an employer, usually their former master, and forced to work for him. Several states enacted laws that allowed courts to declare black parents incapable of supporting or properly raising their children, who were then assigned to white guardians as unpaid labor.

All this happened while Congress was not in session. By the time Congress reconvened in December 1865, President Johnson had reconstructed most of the South. Republicans in Congress were furious. Johnson had put responsibility for Reconstruction back into the hands of white Southerners, who had then reelected the same men who had been leaders before the war. The Republicans were livid about the Black Codes, too, especially since the laws applied only to unemployed black people and not jobless white people. They accused white Southern lawmakers of returning the freed people to slavery.

Some Republicans, the Radical Republicans, accused the president of betraying the sacrifices made by the North during the war. Committed to black rights, the Radical Republicans called Johnson's Reconstruction policies too lenient, and they rushed to change the program. That December, they refused to seat any Southern senator or representative who had been in power during the Confederacy. They also ratified the Thirteenth

President Johnson vehemently opposed Republican plans for Reconstruction. Here, the artist Thomas Nast portrays Johnson as a hypocrite.

Harper's Weekly, October 27, 1866; American Social History Project

Amendment, which abolished slavery, and got busy on legislation to ensure civil rights.

In April 1866 over President Johnson's veto Congress passed a Civil Rights Act. The act made any person born in the United States a citizen (except American Indians) and entitled to rights protected by the United States government. This act further protected the rights of the freed people by invalidating the Black Codes and by granting black people the same rights as white people.

The notion of racial equality was a great insult to white Southern pride. During slavery, the racial rules had been clear. Now some blacks openly challenged the authority of whites. Some dared to sit down in the presence of white people. Some refused to tip their hats to white people or to yield the sidewalk. Some refused to call their former owners "master" and refused to answer to "Uncle" or "boy" or "Auntie" or "Mammy." And some were buying guns and hunting with dogs, something that had been forbidden to most blacks during slavery.

Southern newspapers warned their white readers about the dangers of tolerating such

Outside the galleries of the House of Representatives, men and women cheer at the passage of the Civil Rights Bill in April 1866. The bill granted citizenship to black people and forbade discrimination against them. President Johnson had vetoed the bill, arguing that it "operate[d] in favor of the colored and against the white race."

Harper's Weekly, April 28, 1866; Library of Congress

insolent behavior. In editorials, writers speculated nervously about where all of this freedom and racial equality might lead.

Like many white Southerners, Lester, Crowe, Jones, Kennedy, Reed, and McCord may have discussed the racial tension that hovered like a storm cloud over the South. A race riot in nearby Memphis had erupted in early May, sparked by the collision of two horse-drawn carriages, one driven by a white man, the other by a black man. When police arrested the black driver, black Union soldiers protested. A white mob quickly gathered, and the incident exploded into three days of racial violence. Aided by city police and firemen, white men brutally attacked black people throughout the city, killing forty-six blacks and two whites. White mobs looted and destroyed twelve black schools, four black churches, and hundreds of black homes.

A *Harper's Weekly* reporter blamed rumors for the violence in Memphis, Tennessee. This wood engraving depicts the murder of freedmen.

Harper's Weekly, May 26, 1866; Library of Congress

Afterward, some white Southerners claimed that the black soldiers were drunk and disorderly and that their behavior had provoked the white citizens, who had no choice to protect themselves. Others blamed the North for imposing black soldiers on the South, who symbolized all that the South had lost.

Southern newspapers such as the *Pulaski Citizen* blamed the riot on the laws that barred the most important Confederates—those who held more than $20,000 in taxable property—from voting. "When people abroad condemn Memphis because of the recent outrages," reported the newspaper, "let them remember that the people of Memphis—property holders of this city—have no share, no voice, or vote in municipal government."

But a *Harper's Weekly* reporter blamed rumors that fed upon prejudice for escalating the violence. "During the evening the wildest and most exaggerated reports soon spread throughout the city," wrote the reporter. "Every communicator of the intelligence of the fight told a different story. Each rumor placed a worse aspect upon the affair than the preceding one, and only served to develop the pent-up prejudice against the negro."

During times of crisis or uncertainty, people often resort to rumors, or stories circulated without facts to confirm the truth, to help them cope with anxieties and fears. Of all the rumors, racial and hate rumors are considered the most dangerous because they are divisive and create hostility that can lead to violence.

In view of the Memphis riot and other reports of racial violence, the six men in Pulaski may have spent their evenings discussing the need for patrols. Many white Southerners obsessed about the safety of their families and the security of their property. Many believed that white women weren't safe as long as black men roamed free. These people chose not to remember that many of these same women had taken care of themselves, managing farms and plantations and family businesses, as the men marched off to war.

The six men may have spent their evenings reminiscing about the days before the war or rehashing their war exploits, as soldiers often do. But all that is known is that one May evening in 1866, as the men lounged about the law office, John Lester said suddenly to his friends, "Boys, let us get up a club or society."

The other men quickly agreed and got to work, dividing into two committees. Calvin Jones and Richard Reed were to select a name while the others prepared a formal set of rules.

A week later, the six men met again. Calvin Jones and Richard Reed suggested that the group call themselves Kuklos, a Greek word that means "circle" or "band." Most likely, the men were influenced by Kuklos Adelphon, a popular Southern college fraternity that had disbanded during the war.

The other men liked the suggestion, but they didn't find "Kuklos" mysterious enough. For fraternities that have Greek names, the name often has a secret meaning known only to its initiated members. Perhaps this knowledge inspired James Crowe, who offered a deviation, saying, "Call it *ku klux*."

Someone else suggested adding the word "klan," a word also meaning "band" or "circle," and so they did. In this way, the name Ku Klux Klan was cobbled together, a redundant, alliterative name that meant, simply and ridiculously, "circle circle."

Years later, John Lester would boast about the occult-like power of the mysterious name. "There was a weird potency in the very name Ku Klux Klan," he said. "The sound of it is suggestive of bones rattling together." Had they chosen another name, Lester claimed, the group would never have grown beyond Pulaski.

Several nights after the second meeting, the newly formed Ku Klux Klan met at a large home where one of the men was house-sitting for a family friend. Here they developed rules, closely patterned after the Kuklos Adelphon fraternity. They wrote a vow of secrecy and fashioned secret rites and rituals such as passwords, handshakes, a secret code, and the hazing of new members.

They also created mysterious-sounding titles that assigned a job to each of the six men: Frank McCord was the Grand Cyclops, or president; John Kennedy was Grand Magi, or vice president;

James Crowe was Grand Turk, a master of ceremonies; Calvin Jones and John Lester were Night Hawks, or messengers; and Richard Reed was a Lictor, or sentinel, who guarded the den.

At this mansion in Pulaski, Tennessee, the founding members of the Ku Klux Klan developed the rules and rites of the secret order.

James Welch Patton, *Unionism and Reconstruction in Tennessee, 1860–1869;* reprinted with permission from the University of North Carolina Press

Their organizational work done, the Klansmen raided a linen closet. They pulled white sheets over their heads, cutting two holes for eyes, and another for their mouth. Then they raced outside and leaped astride their horses and swooped through the town streets, whooping and moaning and shrieking like ghosts.

The Ku Klux Klan was born.

"There may be in their conduct some things to regret, and some to condemn; but he who gets a full understanding of their surroundings, social, civil and political, if he is not incapable of noble sentiment, will also find many things to awaken his sympathy and call forth his admiration."

—*John Lester, explaining why the circumstances following surrender justified the formation of the Ku Klux Klan*

CHAPTER 3

"I Was Killed at Chickamauga"

Not long after that first midnight gallop, the six men found a large, abandoned house on a hill not far from the main road leading into Pulaski. The house had been wrecked several months earlier by a cyclone. High winds had left storm-torn trees where a magnificent grove once stood.

"A dreary, desolate uncanny sight it was," wrote John Lester nearly twenty years later. "But it was, in every way most suitable for a den."

Over the coming weeks, the Klan met at their secret den, where they dressed in robes and hoods and then saddled up. They tore through the countryside, crashing summer parties and barbecues—much to the delight of partygoers, who delighted in the silliness of grown men pretending to be ghosts.

One night the ghostly figures crashed a moonlight picnic in a beech grove

Under a full moon, an elaborately costumed Klansman patrols, his gun drawn.

From *A Fool's Errand: By One of the Fools*, by Albion Winegar Tourgée; Tennessee State Library Archives

outside Pulaski. One of the picnickers, a former Confederate captain, was amused at the long flowing white gowns and tall conical hats decorated with spangles and stars. The hats covered their faces, but from behind the white pasteboard, eyes peered out of punched-out holes. "It was a pretty and showy costume," observed Daniel Coleman, who lived across the border in Athens, Alabama.

The shrouded men joined in the dancing, twirling their white robes about them, as if at any moment they might fly. Some romped among the guests, teasing them in low voices that sounded as if they had risen from the grave. Others didn't speak at all but moved about soundlessly, signaling one another with gestures.

The biggest secret about the Klan was its secrecy. "Its mysteriousness was the sensation of the hour," wrote John Lester at a later date. "Every issue of the local paper contained some notice of the strange order."

Notices such as this one appeared in the biweekly *Pulaski Citizen*:

```
Take Notice.--The Ku Klux Klan will assem-
ble at their usual place of rendezvous, "The
Den," on Tuesday night next, exactly at the
hour of midnight, in costume and bearing the
arms of the Klan.
By or of the Grand Cyclops, G. T.
```

The publisher, Luther McCord, claimed to be baffled by the notices he found slipped beneath his office door. "Will any one venture to tell me what it means, if anything at all?" he implored on the front page of the newspaper. "What is a 'Kuklux Klan,' and who is this 'Grand Cyclops' that issues his mysterious and imperative orders? Can any one give us a little light on this subject?"

Chances are Luther McCord already knew the answer, considering that his younger brother was the Klansman Frank McCord.

The newspaper publicity and the antics of the group piqued the curiosity of readers. Soon other Pulaski townsmen asked to join.

Some found their way to the den on their own; the disguised horsemen surprised others at night, blindfolding them and spiriting them away to the den, where the secret initiation took place. Most new members were former Confederate soldiers; at least three were local doctors. Like the six original Pulaski members, these men were active in their churches and shared a Scottish-Irish heritage, one long known for the belief in ghosts and spirits.

The secret initiation consisted of pranks intended to embarrass the initiates. The Grand Cyclops asked the blindfolded initiate absurd questions. Once satisfied with the answers, the Grand Cyclops ordered: "Place him before the royal altar and adorn his head with the regal crown."

A Klansman then led the man to a large mirror, where he placed a huge hat with two enormous donkey ears on the initiate's head. The novice was then told to recite a couplet from the poem "To a Louse" by the Scottish poet Robert Burns:

> O wad some power the giftie gie us
> To see oursels as ithers see us.
> [O would some power the gift to give us
> To see ourselves as others see us.]

Once the novice repeated the words, the Klansman untied the blindfold. As the newest member looked in the mirror, he saw himself looking ridiculous in a donkey hat.

"The den rang with shouts and peals of laughter," said Lester. "And worse than all, as he looked about him, he saw that he was surrounded by men dressed in hideous garb and masks, so that he could not recognize one of them."

That summer, as news of the popular club spread into the surrounding countryside and other parts of Tennessee, more dens quickly sprang up. According to John Lester, the Klansmen were at the time content to play practical jokes on themselves and others. That soon

The two-day battle near Georgia's Chickamauga Creek left 18,454 Confederate soldiers and 16,170 Union soldiers dead. The Confederates won the September 1863 battle.

Library of Congress

changed, however, when they realized that people who passed along the dark and lonely road near their den were frightened by the robed and hooded Lictors, or sentinels, standing guard outside. When these passersby asked who they were, the grim-looking Lictors replied in eerie voices, "A spirit from the other world. I was killed at Chickamauga."

The Klansmen were pleased to find that this answer especially terrified the freed people. One of the most vicious battles of the war had taken place at Chickamauga, Georgia, just a dozen miles below the southeastern Tennessee border.

As the stories about the "ghosts" of the Confederate dead spread, many freed people avoided the places that the Klan dens frequented.

"In this way, the Klan gradually realized the most powerful devices ever constructed for controlling the ignorant and superstitious were in their hands," said Lester.

It was this realization, said Lester, that transformed the social club into a group of bogeymen who controlled the behavior of the former slaves. Just as the slave patrollers had done before Emancipation, the Klan patrolled the country roads, chasing and whipping black people who dared to leave their cabins at night. Some shot their guns at random.

For some black families, it became too dangerous to sleep near

This photograph of an unidentified slave family was taken before Emancipation, when mounted patrols regulated the movement of black people, free and enslaved, after dark. After the war, the Ku Klux Klan continued to use physical and psychological intimidation, just as the antebellum patrollers had. Library of Congress

windows and doors. One woman described how she and her husband and children slept on the cabin floor to shield themselves during the Klan's raid. "Dem Ku Klux just come all around our house at night time and shoot in de doors and de windows," said Ann Ulrich Evans, who lived across the western Tennessee border in Missouri. "Dey never bothered anybody in de daytime. Den some time dey come on in de house, tear up everything on de place, claim dey was looking for somebody. And tell us dey hungry 'cause dey ain't had nothin' to eat since de battle of Shiloh."

Speaking in eerie voices, the Klansmen claimed to be the ghosts of Confederate soldiers who had died in battle and needed water. They paraded about the cabin, showing off "supernatural" powers. They hid collapsible bags beneath their robes that collected the water they pretended to drink by the bucketful. They feigned an ability to dismember, "taking off" an arm or hand that was actually a skeleton bone hidden beneath their sleeves. They stood on stilts or wore tall hats to appear giant-like. Some pretended to be headless, carrying fake heads in their arms.

It's possible that some black people believed in supernatural beings that they called haints, or haunts. Many were the children and grandchildren of Africans, mostly from countries along the West African coast. Their parents and grandparents brought the cultural and religious belief called voodoo to America. Those who practiced voodoo honored the spirit of dead ancestors and believed that they could communicate with the dead through shouts, dance, and song. Some freed people who continued to practice voodoo may have feared that dead Confederate soldiers had returned from the grave to seek revenge.

Slaveholders had long drawn on these African beliefs in order to cultivate a climate of fear among superstitious slaves. Some masters, overseers, and patrollers had dressed up as ghosts to frighten slaves at night and to make them afraid of the dark. For some superstitious slaves, the tricks might have worked.

Most freed people, however, weren't fooled. They knew that the disguised Kukluxers weren't dead masters or Confederate soldiers arisen from the grave. What frightened them were the well-armed, disguised white men who burst into their cabins, outnumbering their victims. As one freedman said, "The reason I was scared was, that they came in with their pistols, and I was afraid they would shoot me."

Most freed people had learned that it was safer to go along with the white men and pretend to believe their tricks so that the Kukluxers would leave them alone and keep the violence from escalating into beatings, shootings, and lynchings.

*   *   *

Klansmen attack a family. The disguised men would soon become known as "Kukluxers" and their violent acts as "kukluxing" and "kukluxism."

Harper's Weekly, February 24, 1872; Library of Congress

Some modern historians accept John Lester's account that the six friends formed the Ku Klux Klan purely as a social club and that the club then broadened into a racist organization that regulated the lives of black people. They claim little evidence indicates that the original Pulaski Klan bullied or seriously terrified anyone during the first summer of its existence.

Other modern historians disagree, saying that kukluxing, as the attacks became called, was nothing new except in name. These historians call it inconceivable that the six men had no racist agenda from the Klan's inception. The six men had grown up at a time when the whipping and bullying of black people was culturally and socially acceptable—and perfectly legal. It seems more probable that in starting their club, these men were finding a way to continue racist behavior widely accepted during the days of slavery.

Still, John Lester claimed that the Klan had no political agenda, even though its growing number of dens were filling with former Confederate soldiers and other white Southern men who had supported the Confederacy. The Klansmen were, according to Lester, "a band of regulators . . . trying to protect property and preserve law and order."

In 1866, as the first Klan dens formed that summer, politics were growing more heated in Washington, especially after Republicans voted to extend the Freedmen's Bureau, over President Johnson's veto.

Congress had established the Freedmen's Bureau in the last days of the war as a temporary government agency to help former slaves and other people in the war-torn South. For one year, the government agency was supposed to provide food, medical care, and education for war refugees of both races and to help negotiate wages, working conditions, and contracts between the freed people and their employers. The new bill extended the agency for three additional years and expanded its responsibilities and powers, providing more financial support for schools, hospitals, and other relief. The bill also gave the bureau more power to defend the rights of the freed people.

The Freedmen's Bureau angered many Democrats who wanted the federal government to stay out of state and local affairs. They agreed with President Johnson, who claimed that the agency aided black people at the expense of white people, especially Southern landowners, who would be forced to pay higher taxes for the social programs. They also worried that the Freedmen's Bureau would fill the heads of the former slaves with the notion that they didn't have to work, that the government would give them handouts.

"It will increase the government patronage to an enormous extent," cried Southern newspapers such as the *Pulaski Citizen* about the Freedmen's Bureau. "It will curse the South with a population of idle and pauper freedmen. It gathers blacks in communities where they are to be supported at public expense."

That fall and winter, President Johnson and Congress continued to clash over ways to rebuild the South. By March 1867, the Republicans wrested control from the president and passed two Reconstruction Acts, which further infuriated the Democrats. (A third Reconstruction Act would

An influential Radical Republican, Charles Sumner, is characterized here giving coins to a black child and ignoring the needs of the white girl. Sumner fought for the establishment of equal rights for black Americans.

Library of Congress

Many poor whites also benefited from the Freedmen's Bureau. Within the first ten months of its creation, nearly eight million rations of flour, corn meal, and sugar were distributed to both black and white families.

From J. T. Trowbridge's *The South: A Tour of Its Battlefields and Ruined Cities;* Library of Congress

follow later that summer, and a fourth act in 1868.)

The first two Reconstruction Acts divided the South into five military districts each under the command of a general. Union troops were stationed throughout the five districts to supervise elections and protect lives and property while new local and state governments were formed. White Southerners protested, arguing that the federal government was utilizing war-time powers in a time of peace.

The Reconstruction Acts also guaranteed Southern black men

the right to vote in elections for state constitutional conventions and in subsequent elections. To white Southerners, this was pure hypocrisy, since at this time only five Northern states granted black men the right to vote. (Women would not win the right to vote until 1920.)

Furthermore, the acts stipulated that no Southern state would gain readmission to the Union or become part of the United States again until it ratified the Fourteenth Amendment. This amendment entitled all persons born or naturalized in the United States to citizenship and equal protection under its laws. Until three-fourths of the Southern states approved the Fourteenth Amendment, military rule would continue.

By the time Congress passed the first two Reconstruction Acts

In March 1867, the Reconstruction Acts divided the South into five military districts, each under the command of a general.

Map by Rachel Newborn

President Johnson pardons Rebels at the White House. Within a few short months after taking office, Johnson granted more than seven thousand special pardons to the most important Confederates. By 1867, few Confederates remained disenfranchised, but to white Southerners, even a few was too many. *Harper's Weekly,* October 27, 1866; Library of Congress

that spring, most Confederates had already taken the loyalty oath or had been pardoned personally by President Andrew Johnson. But the Reconstruction Acts continued to bar some Confederate leaders from voting until the Southern states ratified their new state constitutions. These men and other white Southerners watched angrily as black men registered to vote. Some disenfranchised Confederates vowed to vote anyway.

Men such as famed Confederate calvary general Nathan Bedford Forrest argued that the federal government had overstepped its bounds. "I do not think the Federal Government has the right to disenfranchise any man," said Forrest. "But I believe that the legislatures of the States have." In other words, state governments should have the power to decide who should and should not vote.

Many white Southerners felt betrayed by the Reconstruction Acts. At surrender, they had believed that their political and voting rights were guaranteed. "They considered that good faith had not been kept with them," explained a former Confederate soldier from South Carolina.

Furthermore, the sight of Yankee soldiers on Southern streets

A former slave trader and slave owner, Nathan Bedford Forrest rose to the rank of general during the war. Under his command at Fort Pillow in Tennessee, Confederate soldiers slaughtered black Union troops and their white commander. In an official dispatch, Forrest said, "It is hoped that these facts will demonstrate to the Northern people that negro soldiers cannot cope with Southerners." Never punished during or after the war, Forrest was later pardoned by President Andrew Johnson. Today, historians don't agree on exactly what happened at Fort Pillow: some say the massacre took place after the Union commander surrendered; others say he never surrendered. Most historians agree, however, that, surrender or not, a massacre took place, in every sense of the word.

Library of Congress

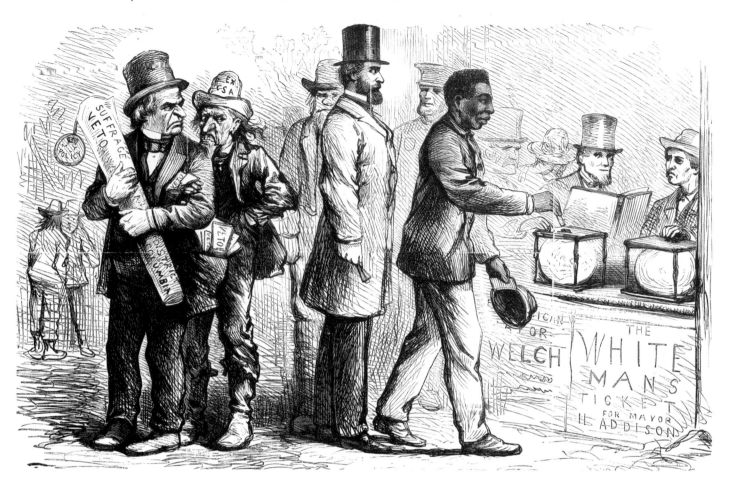

President Johnson and a white Southerner watch angrily as a freedman casts his vote.

Thomas Nast, *Harper's Weekly*, March 16, 1867; American Social History Project

angered many white Southerners, who saw no reason for military rule during peacetime. But a former Union general who traveled throughout the South to assess postwar conditions noted much anger and resentment. "The incorrigibles," he wrote in his report, "still indulge in the swagger and still hope for a time when the Southern Confederacy will achieve its independence."

The general further warned of another class of white Southerners: "Those whose intellects are weak but whose prejudices and impulses are strong and who are apt to be carried along by those who know how to appeal to the latter."

*   *   *

As tempers were reaching a boiling point in Washington, the Klan continued to grow rapidly throughout Tennessee. In April 1867, just one year after the formation of the first den, the Grand Turk or master of ceremonies of the Pulaski dens stopped by the editorial office at the *Pulaski Citizen*.

"Our visitor appeared to be about nine feet high with a most hideous face, and wrapped in an elegant robe of black silk," reported Frank McCord, now an editor at the newspaper. "He wore gloves the color of blood, and carried a magic wand in his hand with which he awed us into submission to any demand he might make."

According to McCord, the Grand Turk commanded him to publish a notice written by the Grand Cyclops. The notice asked the public not to jump to conclusions regarding the secretive nature of the Klan. "Time will fully develop the objects of the 'Kuklux Klan,'" promised the Grand Cyclops. "Until such a development takes place, 'the public' will please be patient."

Little did the *Pulaski Citizen*'s readers know that the Grand Cyclops of the Pulaski dens had invited all other Klan dens to send delegates to a secret meeting in Nashville, Tennessee.

After the formation of the Ku Klux Klan, newspaper articles such as this one appeared regularly in the Pulaski town newspaper. The newspaper was published by Luther McCord, brother of founding Klansman Frank McCord.

Pulaski Citizen, April 19, 1867.

Kuklux Klan.

On last Wednesday night, precisely at the hour of midnight, while we were sitting in our office conversing with several friends, we heard a tap at the door, and in response to our invitation to come in, one of the strangest and most misterious looking specimens of humanity ever seen by mortal man or woman opened the door and solemnly entered our sanctum. It occurred to us at once that this must be the Grand Turk of the Kuklux Klan. We laid hold of the shooting stick and at once placed ourself in a position of defence. Our visitor appeared to be about nine feet high, with a most hideous face, and wrapped in an elegant robe of black silk, which he kept closely folded about his person. He wore gloves the color of blood, and carried a magic wand in his hand with which he awed us into submission to any demand he might make. In a deep coarse voice he inquired if we were the editor. In a weak timid voice we said yes. We tried to say no,—but a wave of his wand compelled us to tell the truth. (A wicked printer in the office suggests that we ought to have a wand waving over us all the time.) Whereupon the mysterious stranger placed his hand under his robe and handed us the communication given below, and without uttering another word bowed himself out.

Mr. Editor:—If everything coming from the much abused "Kuklux Klan" is not to offensive to "the public," or injurious to the interests of your paper, I would be obliged that you would insert this notice

Rendezvous, No. 2.
April 17th, 1867.

"First time dey come to my mama's house at midnight and claim dey sojers done come back from de dead. Dey all dress up in sheets and make up like spirit. Dey groan 'round and say dey been kilt wrongly and come back for justice. One man, he look jus' like ordinary man, but he spring up 'bout eighteen feet high all of a suddent. Another say he so thirsty he ain't have no water since he been kilt at Manassas Junction. . . . Dey tell us what dey gwine do iffen we don't all go back to our massas."

—*Lorenza Ezell, age eighty-seven in this 1937 photograph. Ezell was seventeen when he and his family left their former master's plantation in South Carolina to work elsewhere.* Library of Congress

CHAPTER 4

"Worms Would Have Been Eating Me Now"

The Maxwell House Hotel, shown here circa 1865, served as the meeting place for the Klan's secret reorganization gathering in spring 1867.
Tennessee State Library and Archives

I n April 1867, Klan leaders from all over Tennessee checked in to the Maxwell House, a fancy new hotel in Nashville. Within a few days, nearly every important Tennessee Democrat also arrived in town for the state convention to nominate candidates for the coming fall local and state elections. The seemingly coincidental timing allowed for great secrecy. As the Democrats checked in to Nashville city hotels, no outsiders would know which important party leaders also wore the robes and hoods of the Ku Klux Klan.

Historians agree that the timing of these two meetings was significant. It suggests that Southern Democrats wanted to ally with the

Ku Klux Klan in order to create a secret empire powerful enough to overthrow Republican rule and battle Reconstruction policies. No longer was the Ku Klux Klan a social club. With this secret meeting, they became a paramilitary organization.

In Nashville, Klan leaders called the meeting to order, and busied themselves with the first item of business: to develop the principles that would guide all dens. The Ku Klux Klan outlined its principles in a secret constitution of its own, called a Prescript.

In their creed and preamble, the Klan dedicated themselves to God and to their country, writing, "We, the * * [Ku Klux], reverently acknowledge the majesty and supremacy of the Divine Being, and recognize the goodness and providence of the same. We recognize our relations to the United States Government, and acknowledge the supremacy of its laws."

Klan leaders were so secretive that the words "Ku Klux" do not appear anywhere in the Prescript. Instead, asterisks (* *) signify the two words.

Reprinted in *KKK Report,* Miscellaneous and Florida p. 35

Damnant quod non intelligunt.

PRESCRIPT OF THE * *

What may this mean,
That thou, dead corse, again, in complete steel,
Revisit'st thus the glimpses of the moon,
Making night hideous, and we fools of nature
So horribly to shake our disposition
With thoughts beyond the reaches of our souls?

An' now auld Cloots, I ken ye're thinkin'
A certain *Ghoul* is rantin', drinkin';
Some luckless wight will send him linkin'
      To your black pit;
But, faith! he'll turn a corner jinkin',
      An' cheat you yet.

Amici humani generis.

CREED.

We, the * * , reverently acknowledge the majesty and supremacy of the Divine Being, and recognize the goodness and providence of the same.

PREAMBLE.

We recognize our relations to the United States Government, and acknowledge the supremacy of its laws.

The creed sounds patriotic, but the Ku Klux Klan maintained that America was founded by the white race and for the white race only. In the eyes of the Klan, the Declaration of Independence and the United States Constitution didn't include people of other races. The words "All men are created equal" meant white men, not all men. God intended for white people to exercise authority over other races. Therefore, the Klan considered any laws that granted citizenship and the rights and privileges of citizenship to nonwhites unconstitutional and against God's plan. In other words, American rights and citizenship were intended for white people only.

A scripture lesson is for white children only in this satirical cartoon by Thomas Nast. The cartoon appears in an 1868 book, *Ekkoes from Kentucky*, by David Ross Locke, who comments on the hypocrisy of white supremacists.

> ## INTERDICTION.
>
> ART. XII. The origin, designs, mysteries, and ritual of this   *   shall never be written, but the same shall be communicated orally.
>
> (O tempora! O mores!)
>
> ### REGISTER.
>
> I.—1st. Dismal. 2d. Dark. 3d. Furious. 4th. Portentous. 5th. Wonderful. 6th. Alarming. 7th. Dreadful. 8th. Terrible. 9th. Horrible. 10th. Melancholy. 11th. Mournful. 12th. Dying.
>
> II.—I. White. II. Green. III. Blue. IV. Black. V. Yellow. VI. Crimson. VII. ———.
>
> III.—1. Fearful. 2. Startling. 3. Awful. 4. Woeful. 5. Horrid. 6. Bloody. 7. Doleful. 8. Sorrowful. 9. Hideous. 10. Frightful. 11. Appalling. 12. Lost.

In cryptic newspaper notices, Klan leaders used these code words, called a register, to signify months, days, and hours. For example, an order dated "Dismal Era, Fourth Green Day, Lost Hour" means "January, fourth Monday, twelve o'clock." The register was listed in the Klan's Prescript.

Reprinted in *KKK Report*, Florida and Miscellaneous, p. 41

Klan leaders understood that the Klan's strength depended on absolute loyalty and secrecy. Each member swore never to reveal any information about the order, including its secrets, signs, handshakes, and passwords, and the identities of its members. Klan leaders also created their own mysterious code to represent the months, days, and hours so that no outsider would find out their meeting times.

With its official Prescript complete, the Ku Klux Klan dubbed itself the "Invisible Empire." Clearly expecting the Klan to spread throughout the South, the leaders divided the empire into realms, dominions, and provinces. These boundaries were other words for states, congressional districts, and counties. In essence, the Ku Klux Klan became a country within a country, a shadow government with its own constitution, leaders, laws, and police—all dedicated to the principle that white people only should control all aspects of government and society.

To rule the new boundaries, Klan leaders added more leadership positions with mysterious-sounding titles. A Grand Dragon led each realm (state), assisted by eight Hydras; a Grand Titan headed each dominion (congressional district), assisted by six Furies; and a Grand Giant led each province (county), assisted by four Goblins.

A province or county might have several dens, each headed by a Grand Cyclops, who had two Night Hawks as assistants. Each den had a Grand Magi and Monk, who were second and third in command; a Grand Scribe, or secretary; and a Grand Exchequer, or treasurer. Ordinary Klan members were called Ghouls.

The April 1867 reorganization pleased founding Klan members such as John Lester, who admitted that some newer dens had gotten out of hand, committing terrible acts or outrages that the Klan did not condone. He blamed bad men who had somehow gained membership. "[The Klan leaders] desired on one hand to restrain and control their own members," said Lester. "On the other, to correct evils and promote order in society."

At the convention's end, the Klan delegates returned home. The Klan's Prescript was printed secretly in a small printing office, possibly in Nashville, and copies were forwarded to the Grand Cyclops of each den. Dens were charged $10, about $145 today, for each copy of the Prescript.

By now the Invisible Empire had grown so large, it needed a strong leader. "We chose General Forrest," said James R. Crowe, a founding Klansman.

And so it was said that Nathan Bedford Forrest—the same Nathan Bedford Forrest who believed that the federal government had overstepped its bounds—agreed to command the Invisible Empire. Described as an intimidating man "incapable alike of sympathy or fear," Forrest earned the nickname "Wizard of the Saddle" by his fellow soldiers for his cavalry exploits. Now, as the highest-ranking Klansman, Forrest assumed the office of Grand Wizard, a title no doubt spun from his war days. A council of ten Genii served as his advisors.

Later, Forrest would deny his role, but he would explain the need for a vigilante group such as the Ku Klux Klan to restore order to the war-torn South, even though it meant taking the law into their own hands. "There was a great deal of insecurity felt by the Southern

These three homes illustrate the different economic classes of white Southerners: a wealthy planter's house on the Mississippi River, a farmer's house in Arkansas, and a white laborer's slab hut in Mississippi. Some labor historians argue that wealthy white Southerners welcomed the Klan's violent methods in order to prevent the lower classes—poor whites and blacks—from banding together for higher wages and other opportunities. Library of Congress

people," said Forrest. "Many Northern men were going down there, forming leagues [Republican political clubs] all over the country. The negroes were holding night meetings; were going about; were becoming very insolent; and the Southern people all over the state were becoming very much alarmed."

With Forrest as Grand Wizard, the ranks of the Klan filled with former Confederate soldiers, including generals and cavalrymen who had shared a common bond during the war. The Klan drew members from all classes of men—wealthy planters, small farmers, and poor laborers; doctors and lawyers; judges and sheriffs; merchants; clergy and church members; educated men and illiterate men. These men from diverse backgrounds were united by their belief in limited government, white supremacy, and a fear that white people would suffer personal loss if black people enjoyed the same rights and privileges. They wanted to restore the South to the proper hands.

Forrest insisted that Klan membership was selective: "They admitted no man who was not a gentleman and a man who could be relied upon to act discreetly," said Forrest, "nor men who were in the habit of drinking, boisterous men, or men liable to commit error or wrong, or anything of that sort."

In actuality, the Klan wasn't as selective as Forrest made it sound. "Pretty nigh everybody in our neighborhood belonged to the organization," said W. P. Burnett, a twenty-seven-year-old Klansman from South Carolina who could neither read nor write. "[The leaders] pushed the poor people into it, and made them go [on raids]. I was induced to join, because they came to my house and told me if I didn't, I'd have to pay $5 and take fifty lashes."

Throughout the summer of 1867, the newly reorganized Klan held a series of rallies and parades to show their strength and intimidate the freed people and others who disagreed with their politics.

In Athens, Alabama, Daniel Coleman—the same Daniel Coleman who had seen the Klan at the moonlight picnic—had just stepped off a horse-drawn city streetcar when he spotted nearly one hundred disguised horsemen parading down the street with the precision of a well-disciplined military cavalry.

He liked what he saw. "It was thought that the mystery connected with the organization would produce more terror to [law-breakers]," said Coleman, "and that by riding at night and appearing to be a sort of miraculous persons—spirits and ghosts, and things of the kind—it would have a good effect. That object seemed good."

Local newspapers published flattering accounts of the parades and rallies, describing the ghoulish horsemen as pranksters, and nothing to be taken seriously. The stories made their way to Northern newspapers, stirring the imaginations of the readers. One writer described Klansmen who held dark séances "in caves in the bowels of the earth," where they were surrounded by "rows of skulls, coffins, and their furniture, human skeletons."

Another newspaper romanticized the mysterious Klansmen as caped crusaders, vigilante-type heroes committed to fighting evil-doers. "Wherever a petty tyrant or a great one oppresses the people, there the K.K.K. rears its head," wrote a reporter for the *New York World*. "The idea put forth is that the dead Confederate rises at midnight, and forming into a Pale Brigade, rides forth to redress the wrongs inflicted on those for whom he died."

Some Southern newspapers carried dire warnings known as "coffin notices" to victims. To outsiders, the notices sounded like nonsensical threats:

```
The Sergeant and Scorpion are Ready
Some Shall Weep and Some Shall Pray.
Meet at Skull
For Feast of the Wolf and
Dance of the Muffled Skeletons.
```

Outspoken newspaper editor and Klan leader Ryland Randolph, shown here, wrote of the "galling despotism that broods like a nightmare over these southern states" and the Republicans' intention to "degrade the white man by the establishment of Negro supremacy."

Tennessee State Library and Archives

```
The Death Watch is Set
The Last Hour Cometh.
The Moon is Full.

——————————

Burst your cerements asunder
Meet at the Den of the Glow-Worm
The Guilty Shall be Punished
```

But there was nothing nonsensical about the Klan's very real threats. An Alabama Cyclops bragged about the impact his notice had in Tuscaloosa. "The very night of the day on which these notices made their appearance," said Ryland Randolph, "three notably offensive negro men were dragged out of their beds, escorted to the old bone yard, and thrashed in the regular ante-bellum style until their unnatural nigger pride had a tumble, and humbleness to the white man reigned supreme."

Over the next year, the rallies, parades, and favorable newspaper publicity increased the visibility of the "Invisible Empire," and in turn attracted more members.

Grand Wizard Nathan Bedford Forrest's work as a life insurance representative and railroad investor required extensive travel throughout the South. This gave him ample opportunity to promote the Klan. It was probably no coincidence that Klan notices—and new dens—followed his visits to each Southern state.

Although the Ku Klux Klan admitted white men only, eighteen years and older, women were instrumental in their support, often carrying messages from one den to another, hiding Klansmen from the law and concocting alibis, and preparing meals for the night-riders. Women also sewed the costumes, which ranged from lavish gowns, usually white, red, or black, to cheap facemasks. Some headpieces were elaborately decorated with moons, stars, or horns.

Here artist Thomas Nast depicts the threat that Nathan Bedford Forrest and other white supremacist leaders pose to the lives and rights of black Americans.

Harper's Weekly, September 5, 1868; Library of Congress

In Tipton County, Tennessee, when a white customer happened upon the wives of several known Kukluxers sewing the costumes in the back room of a store, he found himself in trouble with the Klan. "[They] told me that they were watching me, and that they would kill me if they heard of me talking or telling anything," said Jacob Davis.

Klansmen recruited new members, supposedly after a thorough background check. Once approved, the initiates were led, blindfolded, to the meeting place, often in a secluded wooded area or on an abandoned piece of farmland. Some dens met in town in the back rooms of stores; one Florida den met above a drugstore. Amid the costumed men, the initiate knelt and recited the Klan oath.

Klansmen developed a system of passwords to identify members from other dens. For instance, on meeting a stranger, a Klansman might touch his head above his right ear; if the stranger belonged, he returned the signal by touching his head above his left ear. Or a Klansman might touch his right lapel on his coat and say, "Have you a pin?" A fellow Klansmen knew to return the secret gesture by touching his left hand to his left lapel. Upon meeting at night, a Klansman spelled out, "I S-A-Y," to which the other spelled, "N-O-T-H-I-N-G."

Messengers called Night Hawks gathered information about black people who registered to vote, who taught school, who served as pastors, or whom the Klan considered impudent or uppity, as well as white people who voted Republican or broke the laws of racial etiquette by associating with black people and sympathizing with their plight. They also reported white men who abused their wives, who sold liquor on Sundays, and who visited bawdy houses, and, on occasion, boys who didn't mind their mothers.

"The Ku Klux did not consider themselves law-breakers but as law enforcers," said Ryland Randolph, Grand Cyclops of an Alabama den.

At their weekly meetings, Klan members listened to each case and then voted. If the majority voted to punish, a group was chosen to carry out the orders—to either warn, whip, or kill. Generally, a den first warned the victim; a second visit meant a whipping; and a third visit meant death. But these practices varied from den to den, and

The costumes shown here were captured during a raid on a North Carolina den.

From Green Raum's *The Existing Conflict Between Republican Government and Southern Oligarchy*, p. 157

often by the victim's race. Whites were usually warned first, whereas blacks were whipped or outright murdered without warning.

Traveling by horseback, a Klan den might cover twenty-five to thirty miles in one night. "What is called a raid is a night's trip," explained James Justice, a state legislator from North Carolina who was pistol-whipped by several Klansmen. "They may commit twenty violations of law in one night." Justice estimated several hundred acts of Klan violence, or outrages, in his county alone over a twelve-month period, and even greater numbers in the neighboring counties.

On a raid, the Klansmen always outnumbered their victims, sometimes forty or more to one. During the attacks, some Klansmen acted theatrically. Speaking in fake foreign accents or gibberish, they claimed to have come from the moon, risen from a Confederate grave, or traveled from the depths of hell to seek revenge.

Two Alabama Klansmen who threatened a sixty-six-year-old white man wore striped black and white aprons and fake beards and fake mustaches, which they twisted dramatically as they sauntered about the bedroom, sniffing all around the man's bed, as if there were a great odor. The "stink" was Samuel Horton, a Republican who intended to testify against a Democrat. Horton was spending the night before the trial at the judge's house, perhaps for protection.

In a high voice, the first Klansman said, "Is he fat?" to which the second responded in a low voice, "Yes."

"Well, we'll eat him then," said the first.

Although frightened, Horton responded with humor, saying, "Look here, gentlemen, I am getting tolerably old now, and it looks to me like I would be tolerable tough eating."

Fortunately for Horton, the judge intervened and ordered the Klansmen to leave. They did, but later they found Horton again and threatened to whip him if he didn't leave the county.

On a raid, no names were used; each raiding Klansman was assigned a number. They signaled one another with whistles. Three blasts shrilled a warning; four called for help.

In times of need, Klansmen were obligated to help one another. "We were to swear for them, to help them in distress, and everything that way," said John Harrill, twenty-two, from North Carolina. "Even if it meant to swear falsely in court for them."

In addition to secrecy, the order's strength also came from absolute obedience. "We were to obey all the orders," said James Grant, nineteen when he joined a North Carolina den. "When the chief or anybody else wanted anybody whipped or killed, the council was to sit on it and decide what to do with him—whether to whip him, or kill him, or hang him, or gut him, or cut his throat, or drown him, or anything."

Klansmen were sworn to kill informers, even fellow members, who divulged information about the order, its rituals, or its members.

Few photographs exist of the Reconstruction-era Klansmen, but here a South Carolina man models the costume he once wore as a nightrider, fifty years earlier.

James Welch Patton, *Unionism and Reconstruction in Tennessee 1860–1869* (Chapel Hill: University of North Carolina Press, 1934), 175.

Reluctant Klansmen who refused to follow orders or who tried to quit were threatened with a whipping or even death. Once James Grant discovered the Klan's true purpose, he changed his mind about belonging. "I did not believe in whipping a man I had nothing against, and persons with no arms of any description," said Grant, "and I told them I was going to quit them. . . . I had to leave home for fear they would kill me."

Some South Carolina Klansmen would later claim that they were forced to join or joined out of fear. "My neighbors told me I had to go in it, or be whipped in it," said William Jolly, who was seventeen when he joined.

"They told me I had better join for fear of being killed," said Christenberry Tait, a seventeen-year-old Klansman who participated in four raids.

"I was pressed into the order," said Junius Tyndall, nineteen, "for they said we had to keep the negroes down; they said they had to keep them from overrunning the white people." Tyndall went on three raids, attacking black people who planned to hold a dance.

"There was no way to get out of it," said William Owens,

a twenty-five-year-old carriage maker who rode on three raids. "Worms would have been eating me now, I suppose, if I hadn't gone to the meeting."

By 1868 the Ku Klux Klan had spread into every former Confederate state and even Kentucky, a state that had sided with the Union during the war. The greatest number of dens formed in South Carolina, notably the first state to secede from the Union and where the first shot of the Civil War was fired.

In September that year Grand Wizard Nathan Bedford Forrest would boast to a *Cincinnati Commercial* newspaper reporter that membership had topped 550,000 men, with 40,000 in Tennessee alone. If this number is believed, this means that roughly one out of two white Southern men called themselves the Ku Klux Klan.

Five days later, Forrest would recant his estimate, calling it misrepresented. (Other Klansmen would also call it exaggerated.) Although the actual number for the secret organization will never be clear, this much is known: large

The civil rights leader and historian William Edward Burghardt Du Bois (pronounced doo-BOYSS) summed up Reconstruction and the ensuing years in these words: "The slave went free; stood a brief moment in the sun; then moved back again toward slavery."

Schomberg Center for Research in Black Culture, New York Public Library

numbers of white Southerners willingly joined the Ku Klux Klan not because the Klan frightened or intimidated them but because another kind of fear drove them to join.

Today, psychologists explain that people who join groups such as the Ku Klux Klan are insecure and feel a need to belong to something that makes them feel powerful or superior. Perhaps W. E. B. Du Bois, historian and civil rights leader, understood Klansmen best: "These human beings at heart are desperately afraid of something," explained Du Bois. "Of what? Of many things, but usually of losing their jobs, being declassed, degraded, or actually disgraced; of losing their hopes, their savings, their plans for their children; of the actual pangs of hunger, of dirt, of crime."

"I loved the old government in 1861; I love the old Constitution yet. I think it is the best government in the world if administered as it was before the war. I do not hate it; I am opposing now only the radical revolutionaries who are trying to destroy it. I believe that party to be composed, as I know it is in Tennessee, of the worst men on God's earth —men who would hesitate at no crime, and who have only one object in view, to enrich themselves."

—*Nathan Bedford Forrest, as interviewed in the* Cincinnati Commercial, *August 28, 1868, condemning Republicans and their efforts to transform the South and ensure the rights of black Americans*

CHAPTER 5

"They Say a Man Ought Not to Vote"

As new Ku Klux Klan dens spread like wildfire throughout the South, President Andrew Johnson and the Republican-controlled Congress were battling each other over Reconstruction. Unwilling to compromise, the president and Congress fought each other at every turn.

Two years earlier, in 1866, the president had vetoed the Civil Rights Act, a law that declared that all persons born in the United States were citizens. A year later, he vetoed the Reconstruction Acts, laws that allowed freedmen to vote in Southern elections and forced

Uncle Sam, shown here as a pharmacist, urges President Johnson to swallow his medicine, the Fourteenth Amendment. Johnson and many other Democrats believed that the Republicans' "cures" were ruining the country.

Harper's Weekly, October 27, 1866; American Social History Project

the former Confederate states to ratify the Fourteenth Amendment, which granted citizenship and equal protection of the law to the freed people. Both times, Congress overruled the president's vetoes and passed the legislation.

But Johnson wouldn't back down. Determined to fight Congress, Johnson sought other ways to undermine the Republicans' plans to reconstruct the South. He ignored the Reconstruction Acts.

In the five Southern military districts, he limited the power of military commanders, stripping away their ability to protect the lives and property of voters as local and state elections took place. He removed military officers who enforced the laws, and in their place he appointed commanders who allowed disqualified Confederates to vote.

Twice in 1867, Republicans had attempted to bring charges against, or impeach, the president; both times they failed to reach the necessary vote to begin the formal proceedings. In early 1868, Republicans got another chance when Johnson fired a cabinet member whom he considered disloyal. It was no secret that the man, Edwin Stanton, sided with Republicans and opposed the president's lenient policies toward the South.

With this firing, Johnson overstepped, violating the Tenure of Office Act of 1867. This act made it illegal for the president to dismiss

President Johnson is served with a summons to appear for an impeachment hearing before the Senate.

Harper's Weekly, March 28, 1868; Library of Congress

members of his Cabinet without the consent of Congress. A gleeful Congress accused Johnson of "high crimes and misdemeanors." This time, the charge stuck and impeachment proceedings began in February 1868.

The impeachment proceedings angered the Ku Klux Klan. A Virginia den fired off an assassination threat to Thaddeus Stevens, a leading Republican Congressman from Pennsylvania who spearheaded the charges against Johnson and served as one of the prosecutors in the Senate trials. "Your days are numbered, for before the President of the United States is disposed of you will be in hell, where you should have been long ago," the Klan warning read. "This is a free country, and by Heaven! We will not submit to your damnable laws any longer. If we have not the power to remove the laws, we will remove those who make them."

The impeachment of Andrew Johnson was a popular event for spectators. Here is a copy of a ticket to watch the proceedings.

Harper's Weekly, April 4, 1868; Special Collections, Binghamton University

The impeachment proceedings lasted more than three months, but the Senate ultimately acquitted the president by one vote. Although Johnson remained in office, he was a lame duck, politically weakened, with nearly eleven months left in his term.

Republicans now had the power to take over Reconstruction. They pushed forward on their plan to improve the South with factories, railroads, and public schools, and to further transform the lives of the freed people. By the summer of 1868, seven Southern states—Tennessee, Arkansas, Florida, North Carolina, South Carolina, Louisiana, and Alabama—had been readmitted to the Union. (It would take two more years for Virginia, Mississippi, Texas, and Georgia to meet the Reconstruction requirements.)

With the readmission of these seven states, Congress had the requisite number—twenty-eight out of thirty-seven, or three-quarters—needed to ratify the Fourteenth Amendment. In addition to guarantees of citizenship to every person born or naturalized in the United States and equal protection under the law, the amendment also barred any state from taking a person's life, liberty, or property "without due process of the law." And, for the first time, the amendment specified that voters were male. This ratification by Congress was an important protection, for the Supreme Court must honor all amendments. Laws, however, can be overturned more easily.

The country now turned its attention to the fall presidential election between the Republican and former Union general Ulysses S. Grant and the Democrat Horatio Seymour.

Frank Leslie's Illustrated Newspaper typically did not support the Republican Party, but in these two illustrations artist James E. Taylor shows a black American listening to a white candidate lobbying for his vote (top) and registering to vote (bottom).

Frank Leslie's Illustrated Newspaper, November 30, 1867; Library of Congress

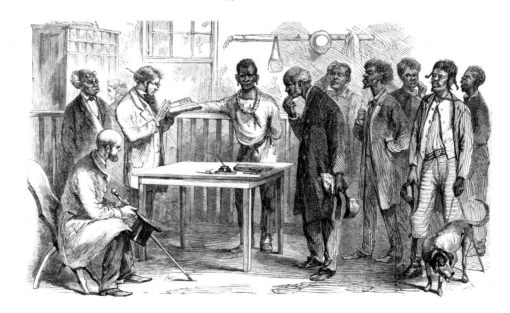

The fall 1868 election would be the first national election since the war's end, and for Southern voters, the first since secession in 1861. It would also mark the first opportunity for freedmen to vote for a president.

Both Republicans and Democrats vied for the freedman's vote. But most black Americans flocked to the Republican Party, the party of Abraham Lincoln that had freed them and secured them the right to vote. "I do believe it [the Republican Party] comes nearer to God's will and universal love and friendship in this world that any other," explained Elias Hill, a black preacher from South Carolina. "I believe the Republican Party advocates what is nearer the laws of God than any other party."

By 1868, nearly every black voter belonged to a Republican political organization such as the Union League, or the Loyal League. These leagues had begun in the North as Republican patriotic clubs during the war and then spread throughout the South after the war. It would be another fifty-two years before women won the right to vote, but women and children attended the meetings and rallies and picnics.

The leagues met in schools and in churches. The meetings provided an opportunity for the freed people to learn about political issues such as taxes, public education, labor, and equal rights. Determined to work within the law, black leaders developed legal strategies to protect themselves and their rights as well as to combat Klan terrorism. They wanted local authorities—sheriffs, police, and elected officials—to enforce the laws equally, regardless of race. "The laws of this State are as good as any man can ask," said the Reverend Charles H. Pearce, a black minister and Republican leader, about Florida. "But I am sorry to say they have not been carried out in many instances."

Republicans nominated Ulysses S. Grant for president, hoping the general would end turmoil in the South. In accepting the nomination, Grant promised to "endeavor to administer all the laws in good faith, with economy, and the view of giving peace, quiet, and protection everywhere." He closed his letter with the words "Let us have peace."

Library of Congress

This 1868 illustration shows newly enfranchised freedmen engaged in a lively political discussion.

William Ludwell Sheppard, *Harper's Weekly,* July 25, 1868; Library of Congress

The freed people were willing to take extreme risks to exercise their right to vote. They understood that voting meant the power to change things. At the league meetings, they learned how to register to vote and how to use the ballot box. At the time, no secret ballot existed; usually multiple paper ballots, also known as party tickets, were printed on large sheets of paper to be cut up later for voters. In some places, different-colored tickets were used for the different parties, thus making it easy for Klansmen to tell for whom a black voter cast his vote. In truth, both Republicans and Democrats tried to keep the other from voting and both practiced voter fraud. But Republicans were not known to resort to violence.

Illiteracy also posed a problem for some voters. In Russell County, Alabama, for instance, a literate freedman campaigning for local office spotted his opponent, a white Democrat, handing out fraudulent tickets to unsuspecting black voters who couldn't read. "He handed one to me and it was headed, 'Republican,' and in the body of it was Democratic nominees," said Burton Long.

Long called the white man on the deception, saying, "Mister, you can't call this a Republican ticket with Democratic nominees." But when he reported the ruse, Long found himself arrested and jailed for perjury. "Everything I possess is now taken from me because of that election."

In 1868, the Democratic Party ran on a platform of white supremacy, arguing that white men had to lead the country. They insisted that the former slaves were unprepared for the responsibilities of citizenship and voting. "I do not think he should be permitted to vote," said a former slave owner from Georgia. "Not because I have any prejudice against him, but because I do not believe he is capable of self-government."

As black suffrage became a reality in the Reconstructed Southern states, many Democratic candidates for local office realized they needed the vote of their former slaves in order to win. Many believed their former slaves would vote for them, the men who had clothed them and fed them and cared for them as slaves.

But they were wrong, as one candidate discovered when he campaigned for the office of state legislator in Georgia. "Realizing that the vote of the ex-slaves would probably mean election for him," said Isaiah Green, "he rode through his plantation trying to get them to vote for him. He was not successful, however, and some families were asked to move off."

Some white landowners encouraged their black workers to attend Democratic rallies. During the rallies, they introduced black Democrats, calling them role models for the freedmen. But this

This 1868 Democratic Campaign badge announces the party's motto and its two candidates: presidential hopeful Horatio Seymour, and vice presidential hopeful Francis P. Blair.

Photographs and Prints Division, Schomberg Center for Research in Black Culture, New York Public Library, Astor, Lenox, and Tilden Foundation

strategy didn't work, for most freedmen viewed these black Democrats as traitors. "We call them enemies to our people," said Robert Gleed, a black state senator from Mississippi. "We ostracize them; we won't associate with them."

As the former slaveholders watched the freedman think for themselves, they grew to resent them and their Union Leagues.

Tension mounted as the 1868 presidential election neared. The Ku Klux Klan launched a reign of terror against Republicans, whom they blamed for ruining the country. They especially detested Unionists, or Southern-born white men who had opposed secession and who now supported voting rights for black men and other Republican policies. They called such men *scalawags,* meaning "scamp" or "scoundrel."

In the eyes of most white Southerners, scalawags were traitors to their country and to their race. "[They] have dishonored the dignity of the white blood," said one Southern Democrat. A Klansman from South Carolina called them "the meanest, most detestable creatures that ever wore the skin of a white man."

In Lincoln County, Tennessee, after the Klan pistol-whipped a white Republican in his midsixties, the victim stood up to his attackers. "My political crime is, I have wronged no man," said William Wyatt. "I have corrupted no man; I have defrauded no man. If God give a man a black skin, I was taught from the cradle not to abuse him, nor tramp on him for what God gave him."

Black men took their lives into their hands when they attended Loyal League meetings or discussed politics. In Maury County, Tennessee, nine Klansmen attacked an eighteen-year-old freedman who had escaped slavery and fought with the Union army. "They whipped me very hard," said Charles Belefont, who was too young to vote. "They said I was a damned nigger and had been a Yankee soldier, and

they were going to kill all that had been in the Yankee Army, or that belonged to the Union League." Among the attackers, Charles recognized his former master, who had served in the Confederate army.

As the attacks continued in Tennessee, the Republican legislature passed a law that, among other things, granted the governor the power to send the state militia into any county to protect citizens and enforce the law.

In response, Nathan Bedford Forrest publicly said he didn't want a war, but he warned that he could raise 40,000 men if Republicans dared to use the militia against the Klan in Tennessee. "I have no powder to burn killing negroes. I intend to kill radicals," said Forrest in an interview to a reporter for the *Cincinnati Commercial*. "There is not a radical leader in this town [Memphis] but is a marked man, and if trouble should break out, none of them would be left alive."

Some employers and landowners fired and evicted workers who voted Republican. Here, a white employer watches as a black man casts his vote.

John T. Trowbridge's A Picture of the Desolated States, 1865–1866. Library of Congress

Freedmen vote for the first time in 1867 local and state elections. In an accompanying article, the artist Alfred Waud wrote, "The freedmen are represented marching to the ballot-box to deposit their first vote, not with expressions of exultation or of defiance of their old masters and present opponents depicted on their countenances, but looking serious and solemn and determined." *Harper's Weekly*, November 16, 1867; Library of Congress

Outspoken black men found themselves in trouble with the Klan. "My daddy charge with bein' a leader 'mongst de niggers," recalled Lorenza Ezell, a former South Carolina slave. "He make speech and 'struct de niggers how to vote for Grant's first 'lection. De Klu Klux want to whip him and he have to sleep in a holler log every night."

But a black editorial writer from Charleston, South Carolina, proclaimed the length to which black voters were willing to go: "If we are to be massacred because we refuse to vote the Democratic ticket; if we are to be murdered in cold blood . . . then let it come—we can die but once."

Such steadfastness alarmed Southern Democrats, who had believed they would be able to control and manipulate black voters just as they had controlled black people during slavery.

Despite the Klan's terror tactics, freedmen turned out to vote in extraordinary numbers. In Spartanburgh County, South Carolina, for instance, freedmen swam rivers, waded streams, and walked miles to reach the polls. "A man can kill me," explained Henry Lipscomb, "but he can't scare me."

It was the same throughout the South. In Apling County, Georgia, one hundred black men armed with rifles, pistols, and clubs walked twelve miles to the county seat to vote. In Yazoo, Mississippi, white men beat black men and women who sported Ulysses S. Grant campaign buttons, but many supporters wore the buttons anyway. Some black women walked twenty miles or more to get a Grant button to wear, defying their worried husbands who knew the danger their wives faced.

In November 1868, Republican Ulysses S. Grant won the presidency, garnering 214 electoral votes to his opponent's 80. A former Union general, Grant symbolized a double Northern victory over the South. His supporters counted on him to end the turmoil and violence in the South.

Black voters also helped to elect hundreds of black and white leaders to local- and state-level offices across the South. This feat

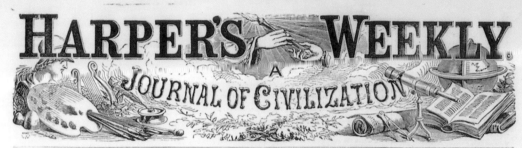

HARPER'S WEEKLY.

A JOURNAL OF CIVILIZATION.

VOL. XII.—No. 620.]   NEW YORK, SATURDAY, NOVEMBER 14, 1868.   [SINGLE COPIES, TEN CENTS.
[$4.00 PER YEAR IN ADVANCE.

Entered according to Act of Congress, in the Year 1868, by Harper & Brothers, in the Clerk's Office of the District Court of the United States, for the Southern District of New York.

A victorious
Ulysses S. Grant
knocks his
opponent, Horatio
Seymour, off a
horse labeled
K.K.K.

Harper's Weekly,
November 14, 1868;
Library of Congress

alarmed many white Southerners, who protested angrily, "The white people of our state will never quietly submit to negro rule."

Like most fear-based rumors, the claim of "Negro rule," or being governed by a black majority, wasn't grounded in fact. In general, the number of elected black officials in a state reflected that state's black population. Over the next decade, 1,465 black men would hold public office, but white men would continue to dominate Southern politics, holding 60 to 85 percent of all offices.

After the 1868 election, the Democrats' disappointment turned to fury as they realized the impact black voters had in the election. It was clear that black political power could pose a threat to white supremacy in the future.

A freedman elected to the South Carolina state legislature explained the reaction of Southern whites. "As soon as they found out they were beaten, they began to get mad," said Henry Johnson. "They have been whipping and thrashing ever since."

To control future elections, one Southern state after another would pass laws to restrict black men and other "undesirables" from voting. One law required that a voter pay a poll tax, or fee, in order to vote. Other laws required that a voter must own a certain amount of taxable property and be able to read and write. In some black precincts, fewer polling places were made available, requiring black voters to travel far distances.

Many of these laws already existed in the North, but a black Southern senator noted the impact that literacy and property qualifications would have in his state. "They say a man ought not to vote, except he can read and write nicely, and owns $250 or $500 worth of real estate," said Robert Meacham from Monticello, Florida. "It would exclude two thirds of the colored people."

But violence remained the method of choice for many white Southerners. Southern Democratic newspapers soon urged readers to organize Ku Klux Klan dens whenever and wherever a Union League formed.

A murdered black voter lies in the street. *Harper's Weekly* published this cartoon, captioned "One Vote Less," by Thomas Nast in two presidential election years, 1868 and 1872, when Grant ran for reelection.

Harper's Weekly, August 8, 1868; Library of Congress

Sometime after Grant's election, Klan leaders again met secretly to revise and amend the order's Prescript, and to formally designate the order as "an institution of Chivalry, Humanity, Mercy, and Patriotism." Among others, Klansmen made these promises:

- to protect the weak, the innocent, and the defenseless from the indignities, wrongs, and outrages of the lawless, the violent, and the brutal; to relieve the injured and the

oppressed; to succor the suffering and the
unfortunate, and especially the widows and
orphans of Confederate soldiers.

- to protect and defend the Constitution of the
United States, and all laws passed in conformity thereto, and to protect the States
and people thereof from all invasion from any
source whatever.

- to aid and assist in the execution of all constitutional laws, and to protect the people
from unlawful seizure, and from trial except
by their peers in conformity to the laws of
the land.

Klan leaders also devised a series of ten questions for each new
member to answer orally. The questions made it clear that the order
expected each new member to dedicate himself to white supremacy:

1st. Have you ever been rejected, upon applica-
tion for membership in the * * * [Ku Klux
Klan], or have you ever been expelled from
the same?

2d. Are you now, or have you ever been a
member of the Radical Republican party,
or either of the organizations known as
the "Loyal League" and the "Grand Army of
the Republic [a Union veteran's organiza-
tion]?"

3d. Are you opposed to the principles and
policy of the Radical party and to the
Loyal League, and the Grand Army of the
Republic, so far as you are informed of
the character and purposes of those organizations?

4th. Did you belong to the Federal army during
the late war, and fight against the South

during the existence of the same?

5th. Are you opposed to negro equality, both social and political?

6th. Are you in favor of a white man's government in this country?

7th. Are you in favor of Constitutional liberty, and a Government of equitable laws instead of a Government of violence and suppression?

8th. Are you in favor of maintaining the Constitutional rights of the South?

9th. Are you in favor of the re-enfranchisement and emancipation of the white men of the South, and the restitution of the Southern people to all their rights, alike proprietary, civil, and political?

10th. Do you believe in the inalienable right of self-preservation of the people against the exercise of arbitrary and unlicensed power?

Over the coming year, state after state would ratify the Fifteenth Amendment, granting all male citizens the right to vote, regardless of color or previous condition of servitude. Congress would also pass additional legislation intended to enforce the Fourteenth and Fifteenth amendments. Called the Enforcement Act, the new law would make it a federal offense to bribe or intimidate voters.

But laws are only as good as they are enforced.

Later, Nathan Bedford Forrest would claim that he had urged the Ku Klux Klan to disband after the presidential election. "I was trying to suppress the outrages," Forrest insisted.

Founding Klansman John Lester would corroborate Forrest's claim, saying that the Grand Wizard had issued General Order No. 1, instructing all Klansmen to burn all Klan regalia and paraphernalia and to desist from any further outrages.

Historians note that Klan activity in Tennessee and Alabama did subside after the 1868 election. Perhaps this shows that as Grand Wizard, Forrest did try to disband the Klan, and if he did, perhaps he desired to restore peace to the South. Or perhaps he wanted to remove himself from responsibility for Kukluxers who had grown out of control.

This much is known: the order was impossible to enforce, given the proliferation of the dens and the propensity of ignorance, fear, and hate to fester and infect and spread on their own.

And spread they did.

This 1870 print by Thomas Kelly celebrates the passage of the Fifteenth Amendment, which guarantees African Americans the right to vote. Vignettes illustrate the rights guaranteed to black Americans, such as the right to attend school, marry, and worship.

Library of Congress

"We was a-sittin' dar befo' de fire, me an' my ol' woman, when we heard a stompin' like a million horses had stopped outside de do' [door]. We tipped to de do' an' peeked out an' whut we seed was so terrible our eyes jes' mos' popped out our haid. Dere was a million hosses all kivered in white, wid dey eyes pokin' out and a settin' on de hosses was men kivered in white too, tall as giants, an' dey eyes was a-pokin' out too."

—*Gabe Hines, nearly one hundred years old in this 1937 photograph, recalling how frightened he and his wife were when the Klansmen appeared outside their Georgia cabin. The Klansmen kidnapped a "carpetbagger" hiding behind the cabin. The carpetbagger was never seen again.*

Library of Congress

CHAPTER 6

"I Am Going to Die on This Land"

For most freed slaves, farming was the work they knew best. As slaves, they had raised most of the cotton, tobacco, rice, sugar, and hemp crops that farmers and planters sold for profit, as well as most of the food grown for the table.

When the government's promise of forty acres and a mule wasn't fulfilled, most freed people had no choice but to continue working for their former master. With the support of the Freedmen's Bureau, many freed people bargained for better working conditions. They refused to work in labor gangs under the supervision of an overseer. They bargained for

For families such as this Georgia one, freedom meant the right to work for themselves and reap the fruit of their own labor and to live together as a family.

Stereograph by J. N. Wilson, Savannah; PR 065-0081-0009, negative no. 50475; Collection of the New York Historical Society

A freedman plows his leased land in South Carolina. For many freed people, sharecropping was an important first step to land ownership and independence from their former masters.

Frank Leslie's Illustrated Newspaper, October 20, 1866; Library of Congress

the right to use the landowner's tools and draft animals. As free workers, they wanted to be treated with dignity and paid for their labor.

Without money to buy land, many freed people sought to rent it, so that they could raise their own food and crops to sell, just as white farmers did. They also wanted to work together as a family, something many hadn't been allowed to do as slaves. Some freedwomen refused to work in the fields, preferring to care for their children and tend their own gardens.

Like many former slaves, George Taylor didn't know his exact age, but figured he was twenty-three when the war ended. He didn't

have land, a house, or money, but he burned with desire to improve daily life for himself and his young wife in Colbert County, Alabama.

"I worked night and day," said George about the first years after freedom. "And had about two or three hundred cords of wood cut, that I got a dollar a cord for; I had men hired to cut the timber laps already down. I was making two or three dollars a day." This was a remarkable achievement for a former slave.

By 1868, George had his own cabin and had started to eke out a living on sixty acres he leased from a white farmer who furnished the stock and feed and seed and would pay George half of the crop. This system of farming was called sharecropping, or tenant farming. Under the sharecropping system, the landowner sold the worker food and supplies such as seed, mules or horses, and permitted him a parcel of land to farm. This arrangement allowed families to work together, setting their own pace and profiting from their own labor. Each sharecropping family kept a share of the crop—usually one-third—and gave the rest to the landowner to sell.

Many white landowners refused to rent land to black people, but others, land rich and money poor, found that sharecropping suited them. The war had devastated their finances, leaving them without cash or sources of credit to pay wages. This form of farming eased their labor problems, providing them with a dependable, year-round work force.

At first, sharecropping seemed a desirable compromise for the freed people and the landowners. It even satisfied racist white Northerners who preferred to keep black labor in the South, thereby reserving the better-paying mine, mill, and factory jobs for white men, women, and children.

But soon sharecropping proved disastrous for many freed people. Although some landowners were fair and honest, others cheated their workers. They set the workers' shares at the lowest possible level and

In Virginia, white men shoot at black workers, driving them off the fields they had harvested, depriving them of wages.

Harper's Weekly, March 23, 1867; General Research Division, New York Public Library, Astor, Lenox, and Tilden Foundation

overcharged them for supplies. With the help of the Ku Klux Klan, they robbed the workers at harvest time, forcing the sharecroppers off the land and keeping the crop for themselves.

The military governor of Virginia reported that some planters killed their workers so they wouldn't have to honor the labor contracts. In most places, it proved futile to arrest the planters. "A gentleman who commits a homicide of that kind gets his gentlemen friends together—and they are nearly all magistrates—and they examine and discharge them," said Governor John Schofield.

Some landowners looked for any infraction, no matter how small, as an excuse not to honor the labor contract. "In the months of August and September mostly," said Robert Meacham, a black state senator from Florida, "when the crops are laid by, the slightest insult, as they call it, or the slightest neglect, is sufficient to turn them off, and according to the contract, they get nothing."

Other planters simply refused to pay, resenting the idea of paying their former slaves. "Old marse said, 'You is all free, but you can work on and make dis crop of corn and cotton; den I will divide up wid you when Christmas comes," said Fred James from Newberry, South Carolina. "Dey all worked, and when Christmas come, marse told us we could get on and shuffle for ourselves, and he didn't give us anything. We had to steal corn out of de crib."

In these instances, the Freedmen's Bureau sent out agents to arrest the planters and farmers. White Southerners resented the way that the bureau sided with the freed people, taking their word against a white man's word. "They listened to every sort of tale that any dissatisfied negro might choose to tell," complained P. T. Sayre, an Alabama planter. "They would send out and arrest white men, bring them in under guard, try them and put them in jail."

But the Freedmen's Bureau could not effectively protect the four million freed slaves from unscrupulous employers or from Klan violence, because Congress never provided enough money or staff to carry out the tasks. At most, the Freedmen's Bureau had only nine hundred agents spread across the eleven Southern states, with often only one agent per county. The agents faced a daunting job, considering one county might have a population of ten thousand to twenty thousand freed people.

Still, in Colbert County, Alabama, where George Taylor lived, sharecropping satisfied him, and he considered the landowner a fair man, saying, "He was as fine a man as I ever lived with in my life."

George was proud of his success. "I had a bargain for two horses and had commenced paying for it," he said, "and bought my meat and sugar and coffee, and had several things in my house which mounted to a heap."

In this optimistic cartoon, a Freedmen's Bureau agent stands between angry whites and blacks, suggesting that the agency can keep tensions from escalating into a race riot. The accompanying editorial praised the agency's work.

Harper's Weekly, July 25, 1868; Library of Congress

For several months, George and his wife managed fine. Aware of the terrible things that Kukluxers did to black men who voted Republican, George registered Democrat, hoping they would leave him alone.

But in January 1869, at about three o'clock one morning, a rapping at the cabin door awakened George and his wife. The next thing they knew, six Klansmen stormed through the door like a tornado. They wore black gowns and white cloth sacks over their heads, with marks drawn for eyebrows and holes cut for eyes and noses. Horns sprouted from the masks.

The men told George they were "just out of the moon" as they dragged him from bed and away from the house. George kicked and fought, but the men overpowered him, pinning him facedown in the dirt and then whipping him, hundreds of strokes, the lash cutting to his backbone.

They gave George three days to leave the county. If he didn't, the Klan warned him, they would return and "put him up," or hang him. Fearing for their lives, George and his wife fled, abandoning their house and the crop, leaving behind all of their belongings.

"My losses, according to my judgment, were over $500 [about $8800 today]," said George later. "I had two mules and sixty acres of land, and all my provisions to last all the year, and never got it."

The attack bewildered George. "I worked and labored hard," he said. "I had married there and behaved myself and never gave any offense at all. They [white people] seemed to think highly of me."

Other black Americans understood kukluxism better. "If they find a Negro that tries to get nervy or have a little bit for himself, they lash him nearly to death and gag him and leave him to do the bes' he can," said W. L. Bost, a former slave from North Carolina.

In county after county, state after state, outrages against successful sharecroppers such as George Taylor occurred as Kukluxers fought to prevent black people from acquiring land and working for themselves. Kukluxers drove black families from their homes, stole their crops, and killed their livestock.

In an odd twist, the Ku Klux Klan added to the economic troubles of the South as they drove off the field hands and sharecroppers that some landowners desperately needed. "The running off of these hands by whippings etc. has driven away our labor," said George Garner, a white farmer from South Carolina. "We cannot get labor to cultivate our farms."

In Choctaw County, Alabama, after four murders in one black community and no arrests, many freed people fled their cabins and farms. "I tell you this [kukluxism] is just ruining that country," said Mack Tinker, who abandoned his crop and hid in the woods for six weeks after the murders. "I don't reckon there is a colored man in ten miles around me who has got any heart to work. I reckon I have as good a crop as the general run of darkeys, and I declare I can't get it.

I have no heart to work all day and then think at night I will be killed."

For victims, there seemed little recourse. Many rural freed people owned hunting guns, good for shooting rabbits and other small game but no match for the Klansmen's service revolvers and powerful Winchester rifles. Those freed people who resisted or defended themselves risked the Klan's revenge on their family.

It also proved futile for Klan victims to report the attacks, since many corrupt sheriffs, justices of the peace, and other local officials belonged to the secret order; those who didn't belong often refused to uphold the law out of fear. When individuals pressed charges and arrests were made, witnesses refused to testify and juries failed to return guilty verdicts, even when presented with clear evidence.

In Mississippi, a black man was whipped for suing his white employer for wages owed him. "They told him that darkeys were

This lithograph reflects the views of most Northerners and the Republican Party: It depicts a white Southerner who refuses to give up white supremacist beliefs, even though he is drowning.

Currier and Ives, Library of Congress

IF HE IS A SOUTHERN GENTLEMAN,

VERDICT, "A GOOD JOKE ON A NIGGER".

The artist Thomas Nast depicts the double standard of justice in the South. No matter how heinous the crime, it was simply a good joke if the perpetrator is a "Southern gentleman." The reason was simple: equal treatment under the law would mean racial equality.

Harper's Weekly, March 23, 1867; New York Public Library, Schomberg Center for Research in Black Culture

through suing white men, getting their rights in that way," said Allen P. Huggins, a white tax collector who sympathized with the free people.

In Alabama, a white man named John Tayloe Coleman received an elaborately penciled coffin notice from the Ku Klux Klan, warning him that he would "pull roape [*sic*]" after he recommended a black man for a job as route agent on a train. "They did not intend to allow no negro route agents, or negro firemen, or negro brakesmen," said Coleman.

The Freedmen's Bureau sent a military officer to investigate the Ku Klux problem in Tennessee. The officer was horrified at what he found throughout the state. "There is no intention or desire on the part of the civil authorities to the community at large to bring the murderers to justice," wrote Joseph W. Gelray. "Those who could will not, and those who would are afraid."

Despite the great risk, black Americans pursued their dream of owning land and becoming independent farmers, often to their peril. In Live Oak, Florida, the Klan attacked a black landowner and his entire family, including his wife and his three young sons and daughter. "They beat my breath clean out of me," said Doc Roundtree. "They said they didn't allow damned niggers to live on land of their own. They gave me orders to go the next morning to my master John Sellers and go to work."

In some parts of the South, Kukluxers drove black families from land that white people wanted for themselves. In Clay County, Florida, Samuel and Hannah Tutson bought three acres of land from their white neighbor and homesteaded an additional 160 acres, planting cotton, corn, and potatoes. Hannah earned extra money doing wash for the neighboring white families.

The K.K.K. sent this coffin notice to John Tayloe Coleman for recommending a black man for a job.

Reprinted in *KKK Report*, John Tayloe Coleman, Alabama, vol. 2, p. 1054

"Dam Your Soul. The Horrible *Sepulchre* and Bloody Moon has at last arrived. Some live to-day to-morrow "*Die.*" We the undersigned understand through our Grand "*Cyclops*" that you have recommended a big Black Nigger for Male agent on our nu rode; wel, sir, Jest you understand in time if he gets on the rode you can make up your mind to pull roape. If you have any thing to say in regard to the Matter, meet the Grand Cyclops and Conclave at Den No. 4 at 12 o'clock midnight, Oct. 1st, 1871.

"When you are in Calera we warn you to hold your tounge and not speak so much with your mouth or otherwise you will be taken on supprise and led out by the Klan and learnt to stretch hemp. Beware. Beware. Beware. Beware.

(Signed)   "PHILLIP ISENBAUM,
                                                                    "*Grand Cyclops.*
                                                          "JOHN BANKSTOWN.
                                                          "ESAU DAVES.
                                                          "MARCUS THOMAS.
                                                          "BLOODY BONES.

"You know who. And all others of the Klan."

Although these men are not wearing Klan disguises, they are participating in similar violence against a freedwoman whose crime was defending herself from an attack by a white girl. Five men whipped her 126 times with a thick rod.

Harper's Weekly, September 14, 1867; General Research Division, New York Public Library, Astor, Lenox, and Tilden Foundation

For two years, the Tutson family made improvements to the land, building a cabin and planting and harvesting two crops. In the spring of 1871, they had just planted their third crop when Byrd Sullivan and several other white men visited Hannah, threatening her to give up the land to another white man, who recognized the land's increased value and wanted it for himself.

But Hannah told him resolutely, "I am going to die on this land."

Infuriated, Byrd Sullivan told Hannah to pay good attention to what he had to say. "You can tell your old man to give it up," he warned, "or in a month's time, or such a matter, they will come here, and the lot will push him out of doors and let you eat this green grass."

Hannah had already lived through worse times, the "red times" of slavery, and she wasn't going to let his threats intimidate her. "In the red times, how many times have they took me and turned my clothes over my head and whipped me?" said Hannah. "I do not care what they do to me now if I can only save my land."

Three weeks later, disguised men forced their way into the Tutsons' cabin in the middle of the night. Samuel and Hannah recognized their attackers right away. The men belonged to the very families for whom Hannah worked. "I had been working and washing for them," said Hannah. "I had not been two weeks from his mother's house, where I had been washing."

Several men pounced on Samuel. He fought back, kicking and punching, but the men overpowered him and dragged him outside and away from the house. One of the men, George McCrea, who was a deputy sheriff, rushed toward Hannah as she clutched her

This 1865 illustration contrasts the reality of Southern black life under the Confederacy with the hope for the freed people's life in the future: a home, education for their children, fair wages, and justice.

Library of Congress

ten-month-old baby in her arms. He grabbed her throat, choking her, and then snatched the baby's foot, yanking the baby out of Hannah's arms. He threw the baby across the room, hurting its leg.

The men grabbed Hannah and carried her to a field, where they tied her to a tree and began to beat her with saddle girths with the buckles on them. "They whipped me from the crown of my head to the soles of my feet," said Hannah. "I was just raw. The blood oozed out through my frock all around my waist, clean through."

When they stopped beating her, four of the men left. George McCrae remained behind, and he raped Hannah before abandoning her. Battered and bloody, Hannah stumbled home, where she found her house torn down and her children gone.

Frantic, she made her way to a neighbor's house. "I told them to give me a light as quick as they could so that I might go back and hunt up my children," said Hannah.

Hannah estimated that she walked twelve miles that night, searching by torchlight for her children. The next day, she had nearly given up in despair when she found them hiding in a field. "My little daughter said that as the baby cried," said Hannah, "she would reach out and pick some gooseberries and put them in its little mouth."

Samuel was whipped terribly too, but survived. Although many Klan victims were too frightened to report the attacks, Hannah reported the men to the town authorities. Several of the attackers were arrested but quickly acquitted. To add insult to injury, Hannah was arrested and fined for filing a false report. She was released from jail after a neighbor pawned the Tutsons' ox and a cart to pay her fine.

"Negroes had to go to school fust and git larnin' so that they would know how to keep some of them white folks from gittin' land 'way from 'em if they did buy it."

—*Jefferson Franklin Henry, age seventy-eight, a former slave and the son of a Georgia sharecropper*

CHAPTER 7

"A Whole Race Trying to Go to School"

As stories about the Klan's violence traveled north, the idea of grown men who dressed up like ghosts to attack innocent people sounded too terrible to believe.

A young Northern schoolteacher had often heard talk about murderous nightriders who called themselves the Ku Klux Klan, but he didn't pay much attention to the stories. "I was inclined for a long time to believe they were like ghost stories," said Cornelius McBride, an immigrant from Belfast, Ireland. "I did not much believe in it."

In 1869 the twenty-three-year-old McBride traveled from Ohio to teach black children in Mississippi, first at a private school and then a public school.

McBride was one of more than four thousand Northern men and women who traveled south to establish

When *Harper's Weekly* published this illustration in spring 1867, the reporter trumpeted optimistically about black schools, "The schools are firmly established and successful, are now seldom interrupted by the rebels." Such statements made Klan violence difficult for Northern readers to believe. *Harper's Weekly*, May 25, 1867; Library of Congress

The Zion School for Colored Children, Charleston, South Carolina, was established in 1865 by the African Methodist Episcopal (AME) Zion Church, which devoted itself to religious, social, and educational causes. By 1866, this school had 850 children and 13 teachers, all of whom were black. *Harper's Weekly*, December 15, 1866; Library of Congress

public schools and teach under the guidance of the Freedmen's Bureau. Many teachers were members of the American Missionary Association. Others were supported by private Northern philanthropic organizations. In all, the Freedmen's Bureau worked with thirty-one religious and twenty secular societies. Together with the Freedmen's Bureau, these organizations contributed nearly $5 million to establish schools in the South.

Most Northern teachers were white and came from middle-class or well-to-do backgrounds. Although some were former Union soldiers, doctors, and nurses, many were white female college students or recent graduates. Most shared a deep religious faith. Many had been abolitionists, fighting against slavery before the war, and a good number came from towns that had been stations along the Underground Railroad.

About 20 percent of the teachers were black men and women, a number that would grow to 50 percent by 1870. A small percentage was former slaves with limited education. Black churches such as the African Methodist Episcopal Church and the African Methodist Episcopal Zion Church also established schools and provided teachers. Despite their great poverty, black communities contributed nearly $1 million of their own hard-earned money to build schools and pay the salaries of their teachers.

When the young Irish immigrant Cornelius McBride arrived in Sparta, Mississippi, a well-to-do planter offered him room and board. In the yard beyond the house, the planter's former slaves lived in one- and two-room cabins. With a place to sleep and eat, Cornelius could focus on lesson plans and his schoolhouse. He had eighty black students so eager to learn that he added additional night classes right away, so that they could attend school after spending the day working in the fields.

With its expanded responsibilities, the Freedmen's Bureau depended on men and women like Cornelius McBride to help them establish public education in the South. It was a daunting task, considering the high illiteracy rate, especially among the former slaves, who had been denied

TO THE Freedmen.

WENDELL PHILLIPS ON LEARNING TO READ AND WRITE.

BOSTON, July 16, 1865.

My Dear Friend:

You ask me what the North thinks about letting the Negro vote. My answer is, *two-thirds* of the North are willing he should vote, and *one* of these *thirds* is determined he *shall* vote, and will not rest till he does. But the opposition is very strong, and I fear we may see it put off for many a year.

Possibly there may be an agreement made, that those who can read and write shall vote, and no others.

Urge, therefore, every colored man *at once* to learn to read and write. His right to vote may very likely depend on that. Let him lose no time, but learn to read and write *at once.*

Yours truly,

Mr. JAMES REDPATH.   WENDELL PHILLIPS.

Wendell Phillips was an abolitionist and agitator who fought for the rights of the freed people.

Library of Congress

"I went to school two winters a little while. I never went full term any time. I had to work and when the busiest time was over I would go to school when I didn't work."

—*Sarah Frances Shaw Graves, age eighty-seven in this 1937 photograph. As a baby, she was sold with her mother to a family in Missouri. Her father remained in Kentucky, never knowing where they were. Sarah and her mother never saw him again.* Library of Congress

education their entire lives. When the war ended, fewer than 5 percent of the former slaves—just 150,000 out of 4 million—could read and write.

Many white Americans had mixed feelings about public education for whites as well as blacks. Some didn't believe education was necessary for everyone, especially the lower classes. This was especially true in the South, where many desperately poor white farmers were illiterate, but it was also true in the North, where public schools were more predominant. Although some whites believed that learning would make the freed people better workers and citizens, others countered that schools weren't necessary for blacks, whose place, they believed, was in the fields or working for whites in jobs that didn't require an education.

Southern landowners agreed. They resented the loss of much-needed field labor, especially at cultivation and harvest times. They needed the children in the fields from early spring when the cotton was planted until the last puff was gleaned in the fall. The more black children who attended school, the fewer that worked in the fields.

Some white Southerners didn't oppose education for the freed people, but they did object to the school's curriculum, saying it undermined the notion of white supremacy. They complained that Northern teachers and missionaries taught subjects such as geography and history from a Yankee point of view and that they filled their lessons with radical Republican ideas about social and racial equality. White Southerners worried that such lessons taught black students to dislike and mistrust their former masters and other white people.

To these whites, the Yankee schools were continuing the war against the vanquished South. "We should teach the negroes ourselves if we do not want them influenced against us by Yankees," wrote Myrta Lockhart Avary from Virginia.

Other white Southerners opposed public education because the schools and teacher salaries were funded by property taxes. These men and women considered education as the responsibility of the family or church, not the state. Traditionally, landowners hired tutors for

SECOND READER. 35

LESSON XV.

cock	wash	pig	too
crows	dawn	dig	two
food	bound	hoe	scrub
wake	clean	plow	bake
home	know	noise	eyes
cheer	knives	kneel	school

What letter is silent in hoe? in clean? Say just, not *jist*; catch, not *cotch*; sit, not *set*; father, not *fader*.

THE FREEDMAN'S HOME.

SEE this home! How neat, how warm, how full of cheer, it looks! It seems as if the sun shone in there all the day long. But it takes more than the light of the sun to make a home bright all the time. Do you know what it is? It is love.

Northern reformers created didactic textbooks such as this *Freedmen's Second Reader* to provide lessons in spelling, reading, pronunciation, and as shown here, a "model" black household.

American Social History Project

their own children or sent them to private schools, and many saw little reason to change. Poor white farmers and laborers who wanted education for their children should get it themselves and not look to taxpayers to provide it, since the burden fell to property owners.

"Every little negro in the county is now going to school and the public pays for it," wrote a disgruntled landowner from Alabama.

Even an essayist for the *Atlantic Monthly,* a northern magazine, sympathized with the landowners. "The piling up of county and town school taxes was like thrusting hands visibly and forcibly into his pockets," wrote William Garrott Brown nearly forty years later.

Indeed, the poverty was shockingly real throughout the South. "We have nothing like it in the North," wrote a Northern teacher from her school in Mobile, Alabama. "The planters have literally nothing left, save the land." But the teacher added, "The people are not more poor than they are rebellious."

A former Union general

This illustration suggests the widespread poverty in the South. Most planters had little or no money to repair the wartime destruction to their land. Here, a white woman sits in despair while in the distance the charred remains of a house or outbuilding can be seen.

Frank Leslie's Illustrated Newspaper, February 23, 1867; Library of Congress

noted the prevailing attitude of landowners toward the cost of educating black Americans: "If the freedmen are to be educated at public expense, let it be done from the treasury of the United States," wrote Carl Schurz in his report. In other words, the North should contribute to the cost of public education in the South.

Some whites warned that education would promote notions of racial equality in black Americans and lead to race mixing. "If we have social equality, we shall have intermarriage, and if we have intermarriage, we shall degenerate; we shall become a race of mulattoes," warned a white Southern man. "We shall be ruled out from the family of white nations."

In the North as well as the South, many whites willingly provided the freed people with clothing and food in order to prevent suffering and death. Yet, despite their charity, many Northern whites were unwilling to provide blacks with schools and teachers. They worried that educated black Americans would move into better jobs

"The history of the world fails to show a higher, purer, and more unselfish class of men and women than those who found their way into the Negro schools. . . . Whenever it is written—and I hope it will be—the part that the Yankee teachers played in the education of the Negroes immediately after the war will make one of the most thrilling parts of the history of this country. The time is not far distant when the whole South will appreciate this service in a way that it has not yet been able to do." —Booker T. Washington, 1901. Born around 1856 into slavery, Washington was emancipated at the end of the war. He worked in the salt and coal mines and attended night school. At sixteen, he walked most of five hundred miles to enter the Hampton Institute, Virginia, a boarding school for black students. He graduated in 1881, around the time this photograph was taken, and was hired to found a teacher-training school for blacks at Tuskegee, Alabama. He became recognized as the United States' foremost black educator.

Library of Congress

and professions, eventually taking jobs away from white people. And, like Southern whites, many feared race-mixing.

Throughout the South, these attitudes toward the public education of black people made teachers and schools targets for violence. At the very least, Northern teachers found themselves snubbed. Some received politely written notes that made it clear they were unwelcome at church and other social functions. Some found it difficult to find rooms to rent and food to buy. With no other place to stay, the teachers boarded with the families of their black students, and this further angered Southern whites.

In Opelika, Alabama, the Ku Klux Klan murdered a freedman named America Tramblies for boarding a white female teacher. "That was the only place she could get to board," said Oscar Judkins, a friend of Tramblies'. "He was an honest, kind-hearted man. . . . The men just walked in and shot him in his bed." No one was ever arrested for the murder.

In 1870, the angry citizens of Patona, Alabama, insisted that a hotel owner evict the "nigger teacher," a white Canadian named William Luke who had been hired by the local railroad company to teach black workers and their families. With nowhere else to live, the former Methodist minister boarded with a black family, causing hostility and speculation among the white community.

Word soon circulated among the three local Klan dens that William Luke was teaching racial equality to his black students. Klan sympathizers began to monitor Luke's school and church lessons. They reported that Luke had told black women that they were equal to white women in God's eyes; that he told his students that black workers should earn the same wages as white workers; and that he had hugged a black woman. This last story grew into a malicious, untrue rumor that Luke had fathered several children with black women.

The rumors incited the Klan, and they demanded that Luke quit teaching. When he didn't, they tried to force him out of town. Once, a mob of Klansmen confronted Luke outside a church in nearby Jacksonville. Another time, they shot out his bedroom window, unaware that he wasn't home.

Luke knew of the terrible things that were happening throughout Alabama, that nightriders were terrorizing the countryside, so emboldened that they didn't even bother wearing masks on their raids. Scarcely a night passed without a beating or a murder. Still, Luke refused to abandon his students and their families. Realizing that the black community couldn't depend on the law for protection, William Luke bought one gross—one hundred and forty-four—pistols on speculation and sold them to the freedmen.

On Saturday, July 9, seventeen-year-old Patrick Craig, who was white, clubbed a black man named Green Little at the nearby Cross Plains railroad depot. When Little fought back, other whites joined in, thrashing him.

William Luke tried to dissuade the men, but they wouldn't listen. That night and the next night, Little and several friends armed themselves with the pistols they had bought from Luke. They returned to Cross Plains, looking for Craig and the other whites who had beaten Little.

On Sunday night, they spotted Craig and his friends outside a church, and a short gunfight ensued. No one was injured, but panic spread among the white residents that the black men planned to burn down the town. The white townsmen formed a posse.

The next day, Monday, July 11, the posse arrested four of the black gunmen and William Luke, after someone pointed him out and said, "There is the man that was there last night." Rumors swept through the town that Luke had told the black men to show the white people of Cross Plains that a black man "could not be whipped with impunity."

That evening in a schoolhouse jammed with angry whites, the local magistrate led a short public inquiry to determine whether Luke and the four prisoners should be held for trial. During the questioning, Luke acknowledged that he had sold guns to the black men. The black defendants admitted that they bought the guns to protect themselves from the Klan.

The magistrate adjourned the interrogation until the next morning and ordered the five prisoners held overnight. Cross Plains had no jail, and so the men were quartered on a store porch. Five men were deputized to guard the prisoners.

Around midnight, three Klan dens met at a Baptist church, where they voted to take the law into their own hands. On horseback, they headed into town and overtook the guards. Realizing his fate, William Luke allegedly told the Klansmen, "I know I've done wrong, but I don't deserve this."

At gunpoint, the Klansmen abducted the five prisoners. Just outside Cross Plains, they lynched the four black men from a tall oak tree, saving Luke for last. Before hanging him, they allowed him to write a letter to his wife, who still lived in Canada with their six children. Taking a pencil and piece of paper from his pocket, Luke wrote:

My Dear Wife:

I die tonight. It has been so determined by those who think I deserve it. God knows I feel myself innocent. I have only sought to educate the negro.

I little thought when leaving you so far away that we should then part forever.

God's will be done! He will be to you a better husband than I have been, and a father to our six little ones.

There is in the company's hands about two hundred dollars of my money; also my trunk and clothes are here.

You can send for them or let Henry come for them as you think best.

God of mercy bless and keep you, my dear, dear wife and children!

Your William

The next day, someone notified three men from Talladega, Alabama, who had known William Luke: the Reverend Henry Edwards Brown, president of Talladega College; Charles Pelham, a Republican judge; and William Savery, a former slave who had helped to establish the first black school in Talladega.

The men traveled to Cross Plains. They found Luke's body lying beneath the oak tree, along with the bodies of the four black men. Brown spotted Luke's letter wedged under a splinter in the top rail of a wooden fence.

They loaded Luke's body into a pine coffin and accompanied it back to Talladega, where Brown officiated at a well-attended funeral. Luke was buried in the black section of the town cemetery. The families of the four black men were not allowed to claim the bodies. Two days after the murders, the men were buried in paupers' graves.

William Luke's tombstone stands in Oak Hill Cemetery, Talladega, Alabama.

Photograph taken by the author

Throughout the South, the Ku Klux Klan singled out blacks who had learned to read and write, calling them "uppity." A Georgia freedwoman who was whipped fifty times for "talking big" and "sassing white ladies" told how the Klan attacked a black schoolteacher's father. "[They] took every book they had and threw them into the fire, and said they would dare any other nigger to have a book in his house," said Caroline Smith.

The Klan also torched countless schools, even those built on private property. Some

The freedmen's school depicted here was burned in the Memphis, Tennessee, riot of May 2, 1866. Similar burnings and other atrocities against teachers occurred throughout the Reconstruction period.

Harper's Weekly, May 26, 1866; Library of Congress

Southern newspapers criticized the violence and arson, but others gleefully reported the episodes, often poking fun.

After fire destroyed two black schoolhouses in two Alabama counties in one night, the Grand Cyclops blamed a comet. "All of its flaming tail dropped off upon three or four negro schoolhouses, set them on fire, and utterly annihilated them," said Ryland Randolph. "The antics of the tail of this wonderful comet have completely de-moralized free-nigger education in these counties; for negroes are so superstitious that they believe it to be a warning for them to stick, hereafter, to 'de shovel and de hoe' and let their dirty-backed primers go."

As whippings occurred nightly in many Southern states, teachers begged for protection. But the widespread Klan violence proved dif-ficult for Republican law enforcement and other officials. By the early 1870s, few federal troops remained in the South, just six thousand soldiers in all, spread among the eleven Klan-infested states, a land area that totaled more than 790,000 square miles.

Even sheriffs with military experience found themselves outmanned and outgunned. "When I gather my posse, I could command the posse, and I could depend upon them," said an Alabama sheriff, a former captain in the Confederate army. "But as soon as I get home, I meet my wife crying, saying that they [the Klan] have been there shooting into the house. When we scatter to our houses, we do not know at what time we are to be shot down; and living with our lives in our hands in this way, we have become disheartened, and do not know what to do."

Some of the greatest opposition to public schools occurred in Mississippi. The *American Missionary* journal reported that one of their teachers received this warning from a Mississippi Ku Klux Klan den:

```
1st quarter, 8th Bloody moon-Ere the next
quarter be gone! Unholy teacher of the
blacks, begone, ere it is too late! Punish-
ment awaits you, and such horrors as no man
ever underwent and lived. The cusped moon
is full of wrath, and as its horns fill the
deadly mixture will fall on your unhallowed
head. Beware! When the Black Cat sleeps we
that are dead and yet live are watching you.
Fool! Adulterer and cursed Hypocrite! The
far-piercing eye of the grand Cyclops is upon
you! Fly the wrath to come,
                              Ku Klux Klan
```

*   *   *

For several months, the young Irish immigrant Cornelius McBride got along well with his white neighbors in Chickasaw County, Mississippi, but he heard terrible stories about the Klan's nightriding in the surrounding counties. Realizing that the raids were growing more frequent and more violent and closer to his schoolhouse, he recorded the details about each outrage in a notebook.

After a schoolhouse burned not far from where Cornelius boarded, and several more local teachers were attacked, his students warned him that the Ku Klux was after him. "I did not pay any attention to it," he said. He also ignored the warnings to close his school. After all, his white neighbors had visited his school, praising his work.

In late March, McBride posted a notice advertising a teacher examination to be held at his school. The examination would qualify teachers to apply for a higher grade of certificate, which would increase their meager salaries.

He understood the implications of the examination: Higher teacher salaries would mean higher property taxes for landowners, and that in turn would infuriate the Klan. "They have to pay for educating people that they do not believe in educating," McBride explained. "They say they are determined not to do it."

This engraving was made from a photograph. Some say the three men are actual Kukluxers captured in Mississippi for the attempted murder of a family; other historians say the men are federal officers wearing the disguises taken from the captured Klansmen.

Harper's Weekly, January 27, 1872; Library of Congress

On Thursday, March 30, several disguised men swarmed into the house where McBride stayed and roused him from bed at gunpoint. The leader said, "You God damned Yankee, come out here."

Instantly, McBride realized these men had not come to whip him. They intended to kill him. McBride assessed the situation quickly: Several Klansmen guarded the three doors to the house. Two others stood astride the window in his room. Realizing he had no chance at the doors, he dove between the two men, through the open window.

Outside, McBride bolted toward a dark cabin, where he knew a black man owned a double-barreled shotgun. McBride dashed inside, but before he had a chance to grab the shotgun, several Klansmen plowed through the doorway and yanked him outside. With their bowie knives and the butt ends of pistols, they struck him, pushing him down the road to an open field.

The Klan leader ordered Cornelius to remove his nightshirt. When Cornelius refused, another man struck him on the head with a pistol, knocking him down. Other men yanked off his nightshirt and began to whip McBride with tied bundles of black gum switches, a kind of stick that stings and raises the flesh. McBride kicked and fought as they whipped him, cutting his back from his neck to his hips. When they stopped, the leader said, "Shooting is too good for this fellow. We will hang him."

In the moonlight, Cornelius spotted a noose suspended from a tree. Mustering his strength, he sprang at the leader and knocked him down. He sped off in the darkness, leaping over a fence and continuing toward the woods. "They swore terribly and fired at me, and the shots went over my head, scattering the leaves all around me," said McBride.

He hid in the woods until he felt safe to make his way to a neighbor's house, where he found refuge. "The blood was running down my back," said McBride.

The next day, Cornelius McBride slung a gun over his shoulder and went to school. Defying the Klan, Cornelius held the examination, as promised, as if nothing had happened. For the next several weeks, he slept in the woods. He was not attacked again.

By the time the Freedmen's Bureau Act expired in 1872, the organization had more than 9,000 teachers working in over 4,000 schools.

A young girl teaches her grandfather on a Georgia plantation.

Alfred Waud, *Harper's Weekly*, November 3, 1866; Library of Congress

More than 250,000 black children were attending school. Admittedly, this number is low, reflecting just 12 percent of the 1.7 million school-aged Southern black children at the time. Comparatively speaking, however, the number is not much lower than the percentage of Southern white children who attended school.

The number reveals that there was far more work to be done in the South—more schools to be built and more teachers to be hired and more opportunities to be made for children to attend school. But the number also reveals that blacks and whites had joined together to lay the groundwork for public education. Despite the Ku Klux Klan's attempt to halt the spread of public schools and the education of black children, students were learning to read and to write and to do sums from brave teachers, and at night the children were teaching their parents and grandparents.

"It was a whole race trying to go to school," noted Booker T. Washington, the former slave who became recognized as the United States' foremost black educator. "Few were too young and none too old, to make the attempt to learn."

"The strongest chains with which the body of a man can be bound are the chains of ignorance. You keep a man ignorant and you've got him. You don't have to stand guard over him with a shotgun. You don't have to lock him up at night. Just turn him aloose and he isn't going any place."

—*William Pickens, born in 1881 to liberated slaves. Pickens graduated from Talladega College, Alabama, and Yale University, Connecticut, and was a foreign language professor and author.*

CHAPTER 8

"They Must Have Somebody to Guide Them"

To see him, it wouldn't seem as though a man such as fifty-two-year-old Elias Hill could pose a threat to white supremacy. Unable to walk or crawl since struck with an illness, possibly polio, at the age of seven, Elias remained about the size of a child, with withered arms and legs.

Family and friends helped to feed and care for Elias. They carried him wherever he went. A friend fitted an armchair on a carryall, a light farm wagon equipped with springs, and in the years following surrender, the dwarf-like Elias Hill could be seen jouncing over the rough country roads, gripping the armchair with his gnarled fingers as his driver drove the horses. They traveled from church to church in upcountry South Carolina, where Elias preached the Gospel and sermons on universal love and scriptural salvation to fellow black Baptists. His bones ached and his jaw was so stiff, it hurt him to move it, and yet he had, it was said, a sonorous voice that rang over the countryside.

Elias Hill was a circuit preacher, meaning that he officiated at several churches, traveling a circuit, or circle, to preach. To Elias and the people he served, freedom meant the freedom to preach and to worship as they pleased. No longer would they have to fear the patrollers as they sneaked out of the slave quarters to worship secretly at night. No longer would they have to sit in segregated pews or in the

Believing that Christian slaves would be easier to control, some plantation owners erected small chapels like the one depicted here. In this engraving, a black preacher, a slave himself, ministers to his fellow slaves under the watchful eye of the planter or white minister on a South Carolina plantation.

Illustrated London News, December 5, 1863; Beck Center, Emory College, Atlanta, Georgia

balconies of their master's churches. No longer would they have to listen to the sermons of a white minister hired by slave owners or a slave owner himself, telling them to be loyal and obedient.

In the years after slavery, many black Americans turned to their churches for comfort and strength. Preachers such as Elias Hill and ordained ministers played a vital role in Reconstruction politics, as they devoted themselves to organizing their communities both spiritually and politically. With the guidance of these men, the churches became the center of the black community and the lives of the freed men, women, and children.

Eager to form their own churches and worship openly among their own people, tens of thousands of freed people withdrew from the bi-racial churches of their former masters. Some held temporary worship services in a "brush arbor," also called a "hush arbor." The arbor was made by cutting a clearing in the woods and cross-tying trees together to fashion the leafy tops into a canopy. Some held services in abandoned warehouses or in one another's cabins. Some shared worship space in white churches.

Some freed people fought for ownership of the white churches they had built as slaves, but most black communities built their own churches, scrimping and saving to do so and to pay the salaries of their own preachers. Most founded Baptist and Methodist churches. Of the Methodist churches, the African Methodist Episcopal and African Methodist Episcopal Zion churches attracted the most members.

Some preachers, including Elias Hill, had been slaves at one time. Others were free blacks, often ordained ministers, who had come from the North as missionaries. Often the most educated men in the black community, the preachers acted as a liaison between the workers and the Freedmen's Bureau and white employers, explaining labor contracts to those freed people who could not read. Many also taught school and were active in the Republican Union Leagues. In addition to preaching, Elias Hill taught reading and writing at a poor black school and served as president of the York County Council of the Republican Union League.

To the black community, the church was more than a church: It was a movement to transform the mind and the spirit of the former slaves. Ministers worked tirelessly to instill in them a sense of racial pride, to encourage them to realize their full potential, and to organize them politically. They saw the things their people needed: work, land, schools, housing, and equal treatment before the law. But in order to achieve these things, they knew that black Americans—and they *were* Americans—needed the vote.

From the pulpit, many ministers spoke out loudly on spiritual and political matters. "It is impossible to separate them here," said the Reverend Charles H. Pearce, a former slave who had purchased his freedom in Maryland, came to Florida as a missionary, and held several political offices after the war. "A man in this state cannot do his whole duty as a minister except he looks out for the political interests of his people. They are like a ship out at sea, and they must have somebody to guide them."

Another former slave humorously noted the political sway that black preachers held among black women. "De colored preachers sure got up de excitement 'mongst de colored women folks," recalled Mack Taylor from South Carolina. "They 'vise them to have nothin' to do wid their husbands if they didn't go to de 'lection box and vote . . . I didn't go, and my wife wouldn't sleep wid me for six months."

At this camp meeting, or revival, black Southerners have gathered to listen to sermons, praise God, and sing gospel hymns. In 1871, Lewis Thompson, a Zion Methodist Church minister in Goshen Hill, South Carolina, found a wide coffin-shaped notice posted to his wooden stand (similar to the one shown here). The note read: "You are not to preach here: a colored man is not to preach in this township. K.K.K." Thompson ignored the threat and was later found dead.

Harper's Weekly, August 10, 1872; Library of Congress

Many ministers performed civic duties, from registering voters to becoming active in the Republican Union League. Although most black ministers didn't aspire to political office, at least 240 black ministers, including some who came South as missionaries after the war, were elected to Southern legislative seats during Reconstruction.

As white Southerners watched the number of black churches

grow rapidly and realized the political influence of their ministers, they continued to worry about being outvoted by the freedmen–or worse. Some were also haunted by an event that took place thirty years before the war, in 1831, when a preacher slave named Nat Turner led a large-scale slave uprising in Virginia. In an attempt to encourage slaves to fight for their freedom, the deeply religious Turner and his followers led a revolt, killing more than sixty white men, women, and children.

The militia captured and executed Turner and sixteen followers, but the rebellion terrorized slaveholders and other whites. Southern lawmakers passed even stricter laws, and slaveholders supervised the religious lives of their slaves very closely.

In 1831 Nat Turner, a slave and religious leader, led his followers to revolt against their slave owners, killing more than sixty whites. In retribution, white men in parts of Virginia and nearby North Carolina killed more than one hundred black people.

Library of Congress

The black worship style evolved into its own distinct form of religious expression, as shown here in this caricatured illustration. Modern scholars describe the worship style as the Christian gospel reworked through African religious beliefs.

Illustrated News, April 30, 1853; Library of Congress

With the Turner rebellion in mind, many white Southerners didn't want black ministers and preachers sermonizing about politics, racial equality, and other matters of civil rights to the freed people. Many believed that these men should serve as spiritual advisors only. "When they have confined themselves entirely to their duties," said H. D. D. Twiggs, a Georgia judge and former lieutenant in the Confederate army, "I think there has been no difficulty."

Many white Southerners also feared the spontaneous and emotional worship style practiced in the black churches, They worried that such venting of emotion—the singing and clapping, the shouts and cries, the dancing and stamping of feet—might lead the freed people to rise up against white people and seek revenge for the years of bondage and other injustices.

Even Northern white clergymen and missionaries found

themselves appalled at the lack of decorum. These whites failed to understand that the former slaves had developed a Christianity that reflected their circumstances, experiences, and worldview, as well as honored their African heritage.

In some parts of the South, fearful whites spread rumors about things that supposedly happened in black churches. In Mobile, Alabama, for instance, a newspaper accused a black preacher of inciting his parishioners to commit "murder, arson, and violence" against whites. "The preacher made frequent allusions to some great conflict which is yet to come off between the whites and the negroes in which the former race is to be exterminated by the latter," claimed the newspaper informant. "He frequently cried out, 'In this hour of blood, who will stand by me?' And his question ever met with most enthusiastic replies of 'I will, bless God!'" The preacher's office was attacked by whites, but the preacher, who was away, was unharmed.

Some Southern whites felt conflicted over who should be allowed to preach to black people. A nineteen-year-old Klansman from North Carolina explained the mixed feelings of his den: "Some of them said they [black people] ought to be allowed to have a preacher of their own," said James Grant. "And that the whites ought not to be allowed to preach to them. Some of them thought they [black people] ought not to be allowed to preach at all."

Throughout the South, the Ku Klux Klan monitored black churches, reporting on the sermons back at the den. In Jacksonville, Florida, Klansmen disguised themselves as women and attended the services. Other times, they stood behind trees across from the church and blatantly shot at black churchgoers.

The Klan also targeted black churches to prevent blacks from holding political meetings at night. On one moonlit night in Tuskegee, Alabama, Klansmen shot and killed three black men and wounded five or six others. The men, church stewards, were holding a late-night meeting to discuss the purchase of a church bell when shots rang out and bullets sprayed their meeting room. The gunmen were never caught.

In many parts of the South, the Ku Klux Klan burned black churches that housed political meetings. "Nearly every colored church and school-house in the county was burned up," noted a white man living in Lee County, Alabama. To protect the churches they had worked hard to build, some freedmen asked Republican candidates to refrain from holding meetings in their churches.

The Klan also targeted white ministers who didn't share their views on race. In Alabama, several Klansmen broke into Moses Sullivan's bedroom and at gunpoint forced the white minister outside, where they held a trial, accusing him of favoring racial equality. Finding him guilty, they beat him severely with hickory sticks. The final blow caught Sullivan above the forehead, breaking the bone. The beating was a warning, they told him. The next time, they promised, they would kill him. Sullivan and his family fled. It took him months to recover from the beating.

Some of the greatest Klan violence against the black church and its preachers took place in York County, South Carolina, where an estimated three out of four

In Huntsville, Alabama, Klansmen drove blacks from Saturday-night worship services. The two men pictured here are modeling Klan disguises captured after the melée that Klansmen called a "parade," that *Harper's Weekly* called "a line of battle," and that modern historians call "a riot." The outrage left two victims dead and two others wounded. Four Klansmen were arrested but allowed to escape by local authorities. *Harper's Weekly*, December 19, 1868; Library of Congress

On September 1, 1868, Alabama Kukluxers published this death threat to a white Southern Republican and a Northern minister from Ohio in the *Tuskaloosa Independent Monitor*. Cyclops Ryland Randolph edited the local newspaper.

Tuskaloosa Independent Monitor, September 1, 1868

white men, including two constables and a mayor, belonged to the forty or more dens.

When the fall 1870 election results showed that Democrats had lost by five hundred votes, the York County Klan exploded with a vengeance, blaming, among other things, black clergy for encouraging their congregants to vote Republican.

The Klan began riding a weekly circuit. Some nights, they fired their guns randomly into cabins. Other nights, they dragged their victims outside, where they beat them, burned them, mutilated them, and murdered them. Some victims were white, but most were black men, women, and children.

The Kukluxers warned their victims not to report the attacks; if they did, they threatened, they would never reach the courthouse alive. They warned witnesses against testifying, threatening bodily harm or that the Klan would have them arrested for perjury.

The violence that drove South Carolina freed people from their homes occurred throughout the South. Here, Louisiana blacks hide from armed whites in a swamp.

Harper's Weekly, May 10, 1873. Library of Congress

Hundreds of terrified black men, women, and children fled their cabins to hide in the woods and the swamps. They slept out in the cold and rain, abandoning their homes and crops, afraid to spend two nights in the same place.

To quell the violence and instill order, South Carolina's Republican governor, Robert K. Scott, chartered several black militia companies and armed them with muskets and rifles and ammunition. In York County, where Elias Hill lived, three black militia companies patrolled the roads, stopping white men to inquire about their business.

Some black men waged a war of retribution, setting fire to property that belonged to white people, burning their barns and gin houses where cotton was stored. "There was scarcely a night passed without a fire in some direction," explained Milus Carroll, a twenty-two-year-old Yorkville Klansman at the time.

In January 1871, after arsonists torched ten or twelve barns and gin houses and one mill during one week's time, the Klan rounded up thirty to forty black men and whipped them, not knowing or caring if the men were innocent of the arson.

Later that month, the Klan posted a warning at a local Yorkville store, the county auditor's office, and other sites throughout the county:

> Headquarters K. K. K.
> January 22, 1871
>
> *Resolved,* That in all cases of incendiarism, ten of the leading colored people and two white sympathizers shall be executed in that vicinity.
>
> That if any armed bands of colored people are found hereafter picketing the roads, the officers of the company to which the pickets belong shall be executed.
>
> That all persons reported as using incendiary language shall be tried by the high court of this order, and be punished at their discretion.
>
> The different offices are charged with the execution of these resolutions.
>
> By order of K.K.K.

Fearful of a massive Klan attack, black leaders in the Clay Hill area attempted to broker a truce. They sent word to prominent white men, asking them to meet. The white men agreed, and on February 11, 1871, the two groups met at Tate's Store, located at a fork in the road about three miles from Elias Hill's home.

At the meeting, the black leaders agreed to cease nighttime political meetings in order to calm white anxieties. In return, the white men pledged to use their influence to curb Klan violence. Feeling hopeful, the black men returned home.

But the Klan broke the truce the very next day, and the raids continued over the coming weeks, increasing in frequency and cruelty. In reprisal, the freedmen burned more gin houses, barns, and mills. Furious, the Klan hunted down black preachers, accusing them of preaching sermons that incited black men to set fire to white-owned property.

That spring, as the raids continued, night after night, Elias Hill lay awake, listening for hoof beats to thunder to his door, wondering if the Klan would come for him. "I thought my pitiful condition would screen me," said Elias.

But it wouldn't. After midnight on May 5, 1871, Elias heard the Klan attack his sister-in-law, whipping her severely in the front yard to make her tell where Elias lived. Next they entered Elias's cabin. They yanked him from bed and dragged him outside by his arms. As they pounded Elias with their fists, they told him he had no honor. "Haven't you been preaching and praying about the Ku Klux?" said one of the men. "Haven't you been preaching political sermons?" and "Didn't you preach against the Ku Klux?"

Elias denied the accusations. They also accused him of writing a letter to his congressman, and Elias replied yes, that he had. He also admitted that he had received a reply.

Hearing that, several Klansmen plundered Elias's cabin, looking for the letter. Others horsewhipped Elias, cutting him to the bone. Afterward, they ordered him to quit preaching and to publish a notice in the newspaper, renouncing all Republicanism and promising never to vote. "Don't pray against us," one of the men warned Elias. "Pray that God may bless and save us."

Despite the severity of the attack, one of the worst blows came later, when Elias realized that not one white man had aided the black community, despite the meeting at the fork in the road. "Those whites that professed to be our friends then have since cried out and rejoiced . . . over our injuries and sufferings," said Elias. "We have lost hope entirely."

During this period, investigators counted at least eleven murders and more than six hundred other brutal attacks. Perhaps the greatest hypocrisy came from white ministers who refused to preach against the Klan, even as they knew that the Klan was whipping and beating and hanging people to death.

Many white ministers shared the views of the Reverend Robert E. Cooper. "I don't preach political sermons at all," explained Cooper, who lived in York County. "I never conceived that I had any right to preach against raidings of that kind. . . . I have no colored people belonging to my congregation at all. My idea is to preach Christ and him crucified, and I try to stick to my text."

Yet even as white clergy such as Robert E. Cooper refused to condemn the Ku Klux Klan, they could not destroy the faith, spirit, and will of black Americans. In June 1871, when ministers and laymen of the African Methodist Episcopal Church in Florida held a convention, they discussed the progress that black Americans had made since the war's end. With great pride, they noted the hard-working families who homesteaded and had small farms. They noted the number of black-owned industries and the growing number of schoolhouses and churches. They also noted that the freed people had nearly three million dollars in savings banks.

These achievements were remarkable considering that most had been slaves just six years earlier. "We proudly point to these facts as a refutation of the slanders by our natural-born enemies, the democrats, that freedmen do not work," said the chairman.

Perhaps it can be said that the great number of Klan attacks shows the ministers' and preachers' resolve to preach freely and to transform the lives of their parishioners. Perhaps the number also shows the resolve of black Americans not to live as they had as slaves.

From the pulpit, black clergy would continue to serve as leaders for social and political change. They would look out for the needs of their people. They would challenge the United States to live up to its creed and promise of freedom and equality for all Americans.

"Sometimes at night us gather 'round the fireplace and pray and sing and cry, but us daren't 'low our white folks know it. Thank the Lawd us can worship where us wants nowadays."

—*Susan Merritt from Texas. Susan was picking cotton the day she learned she was free. She and her husband raised fifteen children on a small farm they worked as sharecroppers. Although Susan never knew her exact age, she figured she was eighty-seven when this photograph was taken in 1937.* Library of Congress

CHAPTER 9

"Forced by Force, to Use Force"

The Klan's nighttime raids in York County, South Carolina, enraged men such as Jim Williams, captain of an all-black militia company. Born into slavery, Jim had escaped to freedom in the last year of the war and fought with the Union army. After the war, he returned home and changed his name from Rainey to Williams.

White people called him Jim Rainey, as if he still belonged to the white Rainey family in York County, South Carolina. Jim and his young wife, Rosy, lived in a small cabin on rented land near Briar Patch, not far from Yorkville.

Jim Williams belonged to a state militia, one of three black companies in York County, and his militia company had ninety-six guns. Real guns. Enfield rifles, sent by South Carolina's Republican governor Robert K. Scott when he chartered the companies two months before the fall 1870 election.

Like Jim Williams, this unnamed man escaped slavery to join the Union army. The artist noted that the soldier risked his life for the privilege of "fighting for the nation which is hereafter pledged to protect him and his." *Harper's Weekly*, July 2, 1864; Library of Congress.

During the fall of 1870, Jim Williams drilled his men every two weeks and every Saturday evening, just as he had learned as a Union soldier. He doled out the practice ammunition sparingly, giving each man just two or three rounds. Jim and his men also patrolled the roads, stopping white men to inquire about their business. This galled the whites, who didn't think they had to explain themselves to anybody, let alone a black man.

A Yorkville lawyer claimed that some of the patrols taunted the white people. "They insulted white people along the road," said William Simpson, "denouncing them occasionally as rebels, saying they had guns and the white people did not have them; that Scott, the governor, did not allow them to have guns."

After the Klan posted its ultimatum on January 22, 1871, promising to round up and kill black men who patrolled the countryside or in retribution for torched barns and gin houses, Jim stationed his militia at the Rose Hotel in Yorkville, the headquarters for the Republican Party. Sensing it was a matter of time before the Klan led a massive raid against the black community, Jim wanted his men ready. He drilled them in the street and increased their patrols on the county roads.

It was a bold move. There was little doubt that Williams realized the effect his black soldiers had on the white residents of Yorkville, that he knew how the white people detested the sight of the black men in blue uniforms—the very blue that Yankee soldiers had worn as they sacked and burned their way from Georgia to South Carolina near the war's end. To many white Southerners, the black militia company symbolized all that the South had lost, and all the indignity and humiliation and racial equality that the North was forcing on the conquered South.

Jim also knew the effect that his company's government-issued guns had on white people. Before the war, white people so feared a slave uprising that in most places black people were not permitted to own a gun, not even to hunt.

When the Klan threatened to take matters into their own hands,

Few newspapers depicted black resistance to the K.K.K., but here is an armed man prepared to retaliate for the white supremacists' violent acts.

Harper's Weekly, October 28, 1876; HarpWeek, LLC

to disarm each and every black man, Jim Williams countered that he wasn't going to allow it. Jim scarcely knew a black family that hadn't been attacked or threatened. Men like Jim knew the importance of taking a stand, or there wouldn't be any place left to stand. And so Jim vowed to his wife Rosy that he wouldn't give up his guns, not without a direct order from the governor himself.

Three days after the Klan's public threat, on January 25, someone fired several gunshots from the Rose Hotel. Moments later, a mill, a barn, and three more cotton gin houses burst into flames on the outskirts of town.

The fires sparked a rumor among the white people that black men had taken over the town and were threatening to burn it down. "Theire [sic] is great excitement to day," wrote Mary Davis Brown in her diary. "The negroes have threattend [sic] to burn York up to night and the men has most all gone to York and they are going to make the negroes give up the guns that Governor Scott gave them."

Certain that the gunfire signaled the arsonists, white residents sent out messengers to other Klan dens, calling for help. Scores of armed Klansmen responded, some from dens as far away as North Carolina. They patrolled the Yorkville streets at night.

Yorkville teetered on the brink of a race war. "Folks were pretty much scared," said James Long, a farm laborer living in York County. "They did not know but what the niggers might come with their arms and kill them."

Jim Williams didn't want such a clash, as was proved when he withdrew his militia from the Rose Hotel. In an attempt to ease the racial tension and dispel white fear, Governor Scott sent an officer to disarm the York County militia. The officer ordered the three black militia companies to relinquish their guns.

The Klansmen took matters into their own hands. Night after night, they rode through the countryside, searching black homes, beating the occupants, and confiscating all weapons. They kept the guns for themselves.

But Jim Williams refused to give up his government-issued guns, perhaps worried that the black community was defenseless against the Klan's powerful rifles, or perhaps because he planned counterresistance. Somehow Jim managed to have more than a dozen militia guns in his possession.

According to Milus Carroll, Jim Williams did himself in the day he rode his mule down the center of the street to the Rose Hotel. There, Williams allegedly stood on the hotel steps and promised that if ever the Ku Klux Klan rode into his neighborhood, very few if any would ride out again.

Soon, it was rumored that Williams had threatened to "kill from the cradle up" before he would give up his guns. As news of Williams's supposed threat traveled, whites grew alarmed. Even Julia Rainey, the widow of Jim's former master, grew concerned. Was this the Jim she had known his entire life? The Jim who had been her carriage driver? Who had so often visited her home after the war, sitting in her kitchen, chatting comfortably?

"He always felt at liberty to enter my kitchen at any time to see the old family servant," said Julia Rainey. "There was always a great deal of politeness between us, and therefore [I] saw and heard a great deal of him." But now, Rainey admitted, she feared Jim and his "disorderly" band of men.

It will never be known if Jim Williams threatened an impending massacre or if the Klan fabricated the rumor to justify its actions. But later that day, the very day that Williams had stood on the hotel steps, three York County Klan dens hatched plans to raid his cabin, come the first Monday in March.

Later, Klansman Milus Carroll would simply say, "He and his company became a nuisance to the surrounding country."

That Monday, March 6, 1871, the three dens met at Briar Patch. It was two o'clock in the morning, and under the bright moon about forty men stood, wearing red or white gowns with black hoods.

In the spill of moonlight, they initiated several new members, including sixteen-year-old Sam Ferguson, who knelt and recited the Klan oath. No one knew the full extent of the plot, except the Grand Cyclops, James Rufus Bratton, a local physician, who had known Jim his entire life.

Milus Carroll led the way to the Williams cabin. Reaching the small dark house, the men called for Jim Rainey, using his slave name. They waited a few minutes and then forced open the wooden door, cracking it as they stormed inside.

Rosy Williams pleaded with the men, telling them her husband wasn't home, that Jim had left and she didn't know where he had gone. Bratton ordered the Klansmen to pry up the wooden floorboards.

Someone held up a torch. There, in the darkness below, crouched Jim Williams. Several men grabbed Jim and hauled him outside, where Bratton tied a rope around his neck.

As Rosy heard Jim struggling, making sounds as if he was strangling, she begged the men not to hurt her husband. But the Klansmen growled at her to shut the door and go to bed. Rosy closed the door, fearing for her life and for Jim's. Through a crack, she watched as they dragged Jim across the yard and into the woods, until she could see them no longer.

That night Rosy paced the cabin. She didn't go for help, perhaps out of fear or perhaps because she knew no one could save her husband now. Anybody who was somebody in town, from the local doctors to the sheriff, was a Klansman. The nearest telegraph office was in the town of Chester, nearly twenty miles away, and its telegraph operator was a known Klansman.

The next morning, Rosy mustered her courage to search for Jim. "I was scared," said Rosy. "Then I went for my people. To get someone to go help me look for him; and I met an old man who told me they had found him, and said he was dead. They had hung him."

Fifty-three years later, Milus Carroll would reveal gruesome facts about the murder: how Jim had fought for his life; how he had pleaded and prayed; how, with the rope around his neck, he scrambled up the tall pine out of reach; how a Klansman climbed up after him and pushed him, and when Jim clung to the thick limb, the Klansman hacked at his fingers with a knife, forcing Jim to drop.

"He died cursing, pleading, and praying all in one breath," said Milus Carroll. In a final affront, Bratton pinned a paper to Williams's shirt. It said, "Capt. Jim Williams on his big muster."

The murder sent another wave of fear throughout the black community. For two days Jim's militia company threatened to kill all white men. But in the end, they didn't retaliate.

On March 9, 1871, three days after the murder of Jim Williams, the Klan published a notice in the *Yorkville Enquirer,* declaring boldly: "The intelligent, honest white people (the tax-payers) of this county shall rule it! We can no longer put up with negro rule, black bayonets, and a miserably degraded and thievish set of lawmakers (God save the mark!), the scum of the earth, the scrapings of creation. We are pledged to stop it; we are determined to end it, even if we are 'forced by force, to use force.'"

Reports of these atrocities and countless others poured into President Grant's office and before Congress. From Nashville, Tennessee, the president and Congress heard about Republicans who were whipped, maltreated, and shot, and driven into hiding out of fear for their lives.

Thomas Nast called this illustration "Southern Justice." Here, Nast depicts two victims of a lynch mob: a black man, left, and a white Yankee, right, and a crowd of onlookers including a small child.

Harper's Weekly, March 23, 1867; Library of Congress.

From Alabama they heard the schoolteacher William Luke's last letter to his wife, written minutes before he was hanged by the Klan.

From Meridian, Mississippi, they heard about a white judge and seven black witnesses who were shot and killed in a courtroom; an eighth black witness who survived the shooting was hurled to his death from a second-floor window. From Kentucky, where the state was described as a "smoldering volcano," they heard from freedmen who wrote to Congress, begging for protection from the Klan. From North Carolina, they heard from a former Klansman himself, who admitted that the "Lost Cause" was still being fought, underground. The Klan's objective, said this witness, was to overthrow Reconstruction policies and to prevent black men from voting.

Other reports came from federal military officers such as Major Lewis M. Merrill who had witnessed the terror and violence in South Carolina firsthand. But under the laws of the United States Constitution, Merrill and his federal troops could not intercede unless the local and state authorities asked for help.

In his long reports to the adjutant general, Merrill cited outrage after outrage and vented his frustration. "It requires great patience and self-control to keep ones [*sic*] hands off these infamous cowards," he wrote, "when absolute knowledge exists of who they are, and what they do, and what they propose to do."

At last, President Grant realized something that thousands of Klan victims had long known: that life and property were in peril and that justice was impossible in Southern local and state courts. The Klan's influence and corruption were too widespread. "That the power to correct these evils is beyond the control of the State authorities, I do not doubt," wrote President Grant in a message to Congress.

But as Major Merrill had lamented, the United States Constitution limited the federal government's power to use federal soldiers against any state. In order to deploy federal troops to a state such as South Carolina, the federal government had to give itself the right to intervene.

That's just what President Grant intended to do.

In April, President Grant signed the Civil Rights Act of 1871, better known as the Ku Klux Klan Act. This new law enforced the Fourteenth Amendment, which had been ratified nearly three years earlier in 1868. The Ku Klux Klan Act made it a federal offense to interfere with an individual's right to vote, hold office, serve on a jury, or enjoy equal protection of the law.

The act also made it illegal for groups to conspire together or wear disguises to intimidate or harm individuals or to hinder state authorities from protecting citizens. Those groups or individuals accused of doing these things would be tried in a federal court, not in local or state courts.

In cases of extreme violence, the act authorized the president to send in federal troops and to suspend the writ of habeas corpus—or the right to be brought before a judge and not be arrested and jailed and held for trial without evidence. This would allow the federal government to move quickly, making mass arrests. Otherwise, each arrest would have to be backed with formal charges.

On April 20, 1871, President Ulysses S. Grant signed the Civil Rights Act of 1871, better known as the Ku Klux Klan Act.

Frank Leslie's Illustrated Newspaper, May 13, 1871; Library of Congress

This last piece of legislation incensed Democrats, who argued that the new law was "unlawful seizure" and was a direct violation of the United States Constitution, which said that "the privilege of the writ of habeas corpus shall not be suspended." But the Constitution also stated: "unless when in cases of rebellion or invasion or the public safety may require it."

Democrats insisted the Klan reports were exaggerated and there was no need to legislate against a "myth." They called the new laws dire threats to individual freedom. A Southern woman complained bitterly about such "unlawful seizure." "White men would be arrested on blank warrants or no warrant at all," wrote Myrta Lockett Avary, "carried long distances from home, held for weeks or months, and then be released without ever being brought to trial."

But leading Republicans defended the legislation. "If the Federal Government cannot pass laws to protect the rights, liberty, and lives of citizens of the United States in the States," asked Benjamin Butler, a member of the House of Representatives who had authored the legislation, "why were guarantees of those fundamental rights put in the Constitution at all?"

At last, with the Ku Klux Klan acts in place, President Grant and the federal government had the power and authority to move against the Klan.

"And I want to say further that the K.K.K. saved our State from ruin and that it has had a wholesome influence over the lawless element up to the present time."

—*Milius S. Carroll, in 1924. As a South Carolina Klansman, Carroll participated in the murderous raid on Jim Williams in 1871.*

CHAPTER 10

"The Sacredness of the Human Person"

President Grant sent undercover detectives to the Klan-infested states. Pretending to be businessmen or men looking for work, the detectives infiltrated the order. They uncovered names and other secret information about the Klan, from signs to passwords to codes to even their secret cry for help: "Avalanche." They dashed their reports across telegraph wires to the president.

Although the federal government now had the power to use force, the Justice Department hoped to use legal means to break up the Klan. They wanted to prove that the United States was a nation of laws, and that its laws would work to arrest, hold trials, and punish the guilty—if enforced. The Justice Department intended to use federal soldiers only as a last resort to help local authorities make arrests.

To set their plan in motion, the Justice Department authorized a joint committee of seven senators and fourteen representatives, both Republicans and Democrats, to investigate conditions in the Southern states. This joint committee sent subcommittees to South Carolina, North Carolina, Georgia, Florida, Tennessee, Alabama, and Mississippi, where the Klan was considered most virulent. Only minimal effort was made to gather evidence from Louisiana, Arkansas, Texas, Virginia, and Tennessee. No effort was made in Kentucky.

For the next eight months, from May through December 1871, the subcommittees gathered testimony from witnesses from all walks

The Ku Klux Klan Act empowered federal authorities to intervene in local and state affairs. In August 1871, a North Carolina den sentenced the Republican John Campbell (pictured here) to death. Fortunately, a U.S. marshal and federal soldiers arrived in time to save the condemned man and arrest the Klansmen.

Frank Leslie's Illustrated Newspaper, October 7, 1871; Library of Congress

of life: Klansmen and victims; Republicans and Democrats; planters, farmers, and poor whites; the educated and the uneducated; preachers and teachers; blacks and whites, male and female; adults, teenagers, and children. The youngest Klansman, the son of a South Carolina Klan leader who inducted him before taking him on a raid, was thirteen.

Each witness was examined and cross-examined during public hearings. Newspaper reporters quoted the witnesses and summarized their testimony. For weeks, Northern readers followed the trials closely, shocked at the extent and horror of the violence.

In Clay County, Florida, when the freedman Samuel Tutson and his wife, Hannah, learned about the investigation, they took their land title and headed to the county seat, Green Cove Springs, where they had heard they could find a United States lawyer.

There, someone pointed the Tutsons to a public bathhouse. They stood outside until several important-looking white men emerged. "Isn't one of you gentlemen a United States lawyer?" asked Samuel Tutson. When one of the men responded yes, Samuel showed him the land title and told him how Kukluxers had beat him and his wife, trying to force them from the land they had owned and worked for three years.

Three weeks later, Samuel and Hannah sat in a Jacksonville, Florida, courthouse, testifying before the congressional sub-committee. They recounted the brutal attack and told how no arrests had been made.

In state after state throughout the South, hundreds of freed people like the Tutsons stepped forward to tell their stories. It took great courage, for no witnesses knew what awaited them after testifying, whether they would be evicted or fired, or beaten or killed.

Still they came forward. Some, such as Henry Lipscomb from South Carolina, told how men whom they had known their entire lives attacked them. Henry's seventy-five-year-old brother described the crippling beating he suffered and how he had lost the greatest part of his crop. He told of his own fear and the terror that permeated the black communities. "They are afraid to stay in their houses of a night," said Daniel Lipscomb. "If I hear a stick crack, I am watching to see them come and take me. . . . I have been stung once, and a burnt child fears the fire."

In Alabama, George Taylor told the court how he and his wife lost all that they had owned after the Klan forced them out of their home and off their land, leaving a substantial crop in the ground, provisions enough to last the year, two mules, and a horse that George had bargained for.

In Yorkville, South Carolina, the crippled preacher Elias Hill whispered the names of his attackers out of fear they might hear. He described the devastating effect the Klan's raids had on him and the black community. "We do not believe it possible, from the past history and present aspect of affairs, for our people to live in this country peaceably, and educate and elevate their children to that degree which they desire," said Elias. "They do not believe it possible—neither do I."

Later that fall, Elias Hill and 167 other former slaves would board a ship and sail for Liberia, a free republic founded in 1847 on the western coast of Africa. Its founders, the American Colonization Society, believed that white prejudice would never allow black people to enjoy full citizenship in the United States.

In Columbia, South Carolina, Rosy Williams described how Jim hadn't wanted to relinquish his guns, how the Klan had raided their cabin, and how they had tied a rope around her husband's neck. She told how the Klan dragged Jim into the woods, and how the next day, she found his body hanging from a pine tree. But the widow was discharged as a witness after the defense counsel objected to her testimony about the guns as "hearsay."

Cornelius McBride, the white schoolteacher from Mississippi, carried his notebooks to Washington. Relying on his notes, McBride provided eighteen pages of testimony about the Klan's raids against

These freed people from Arkansas await transportation to Liberia, Africa, where they hope to own land and lead independent lives, a dream they no longer considered possible in the United States. Most black Americans, however, refused to surrender their claim to United States citizenship and equal rights. "We are not Africans now, but colored Americans, and are entitled to American citizenship," wrote one man in 1877.

Frank Leslie's Illustrated Newspaper, April 24, 1880; Library of Congress

teachers and freed people in Sparta, Mississippi, and nearby counties, recounting each violent episode in detail.

He explained how fear kept victims from pressing charges. "I was the only one that attempted it," said McBride, "and I risked my life in doing it. I knew that I was playing a game of life and death in doing it; that those men would kill me if they could."

To the committee, McBride summarized the sort of men who

joined the Ku Klux Klan. "As a general thing, they are an ignorant, illiterate set of men, and they seem determined to keep everybody else the same."

To the most violent regions, President Grant dispatched U.S. marshals and federal soldiers to deal with the nightriders. Using his new authority, Grant suspended the writ of habeas corpus in nine South Carolina counties so that suspected Klansmen could be arrested and jailed in mass numbers without a wait for evidence.

The South Carolina Klansmen were ordered to surrender their arms and disguises. As federal marshals and their troops closed in, hundreds of the South Carolina Klansmen surrendered. In some cases, entire dens surrendered together. Many pleaded guilty and agreed to testify in return for immunity or light sentences. The Klan called these men "pukers." Some dens swore revenge on pukers and others who testified against the Klan.

Throughout the South, thousands of Klansmen fled. In South Carolina alone, an estimated two thousand Klansmen escaped to Canada. Among these fugitives were two prominent York County physicians: James Rufus Bratton, who had organized the murderous raid on Jim Williams, and Edward Avery, who had led another brutal attack on a black preacher. Their friends claimed that it was impossible that good citizens such as the two doctors could have committed such crimes and that the two doctors were only fleeing from despotism.

Democrats reacted with great indignation and hostility toward the mass arrests and prosecutions. They condemned the victims' stories as lies or distortions of the truth. Some accused the victims of provoking the attacks. In Alabama, a U.S congressman told how the Patona residents blamed William Luke for the hostility he had aroused, especially among the leaders of the local Klan dens. "Luke had made himself particularly obnoxious," said Peter Dox, a Democrat. "He was a miscegenationist [*sic*]. . . . That doctrine is very offensive among those mountaineers."

Other witnesses argued that the Klansmen were reluctant regulators who had taken the law into their own hands in order to prevent or punish political corruption. Unfortunately, the charges of corruption were often true. Throughout the Reconstruction years, many Republican officials, black and white, had engaged in fraudulent activities, from voter fraud to moneymaking schemes. So had Democrats.

Without the funds or the staff to prosecute the thousands of Klansmen, the prosecutors concentrated on Klan leaders. Some Klan leaders, such as Nathan Bedford Forrest, were granted immunity in exchange for their testimony.

Despite the immunity, Forrest evaded the questions, often claiming he didn't know. Although men who knew Forrest well credited him with a quick mind and a good memory, Forrest repeatedly told the prosecutor, "I do not remember" and "I do not recall."

He refused to admit his role in the Klan, but he justified the order's vigilante violence, arguing that Klansmen defended the South against Northern Republican aggression and from outrages committed by black people. "I think this organization was got up to protect the weak," said Forrest, "with no political intention at all."

When the prosecutor asked about the *Cincinnati Commercial* newspaper interview in which Forrest revealed that the Klan numbered about 550,000 men, Forrest again blamed the reporter. "The whole statement is wrong, he did not give anything as it took place," said Forrest under oath. "So far as numbers were concerned I knew nothing about the numbers of the organization. . . . I knew nothing about its operations."

Forrest claimed that he learned about the Ku Klux Klan from "information from others." Yet when pressed for the names of those people, he said that one was dead and that he couldn't recall the names of the others.

But Forrest took credit for urging the Ku Klux Klan to disband after the presidential election of 1868. "I talked with different people that I believed were connected with it, and urged its disbandment, that it should be broken up," said Forrest. "My object was to keep peace."

There was little doubt that Forrest knew more than he told and that the famous cavalry general had outmaneuvered the prosecutor. Afterward, in a bar, Forrest allegedly told a friend, "I've been lying like a gentleman." The Congressional investigating committee would ultimately decide in Forrest's favor, finding no evidence that he had founded or led the Klan.

Just a few months earlier, black men, women, and children had hidden in the South Carolina woods and swamps, out of fear for the Klan. Now, hundreds of South Carolina Klansmen hid in the woods to avoid arrest. Several hundred others testified or pleaded guilty in return for immunity or light treatment, which was given to men such as Milus Carroll, who admitted to the raid on Jim Williams but denied knowing who had murdered him. Carroll was fined one hundred dollars and sentenced to eighteen months.

Many Klansmen in their late teens and early twenties blamed their lack of education, which one judge described as "deplorable ignorance." These men claimed they had been duped into joining, saying it was customary for poor men like themselves to follow orders from the leading men in the communities.

Some South Carolina Klansmen such as William Self sounded remorseful. "I know I done wrong," Self told the judge. "I was ordered to do it by the Klan; of course, I didn't feel like it was right." The judge called William Self's conduct "unmanly" and sentenced him to three months, including time already "suffered."

Others seemed unrepentant or unable to see what they had done was wrong. After nineteen-year old Frederick Harris confessed to five raids, naming the black men that he and his den had pulled from bed and whipped, Judge Hugh Bond asked, "Would you not have thought it wrong if James Gaffney [one of the victims] had dragged you out of bed and whipped you?"

"Well," said Harris, "I suppose I would have thought hard of it."

"Don't you suppose he thought the same?"

"I didn't know whether it was wrong or not," answered Harris. "I was ordered to do it by the committee."

Judge Hugh Bond was appalled at the lack of empathy and remorse and conscience in the Klansmen who stood before him. "None of you seems to have the slightest idea of, or respect for, the sacredness of the human person," he told them.

The judge told the Klansmen that they had to make a choice: either to be ignorant and follow the laws of the Ku Klux Klan or to be men and follow the laws of the United States. "They cannot exist together," said Judge Bond about the choices. "And it only needs a little manliness and courage on the part of you ignorant dupes of designing men to give supremacy to the law."

"Every man has to serve God under his own vine and fig tree."

—*Martin Jackson, recalling this advice from his father, 1937. In other words, his father is saying that the full promise of freedom is a person's right to work for himself and to reap the fruits of his own labor without fear. Martin Jackson, born a slave in 1847, is shown here at age ninety.* Library of Congress

"It Tuck a Long Time"

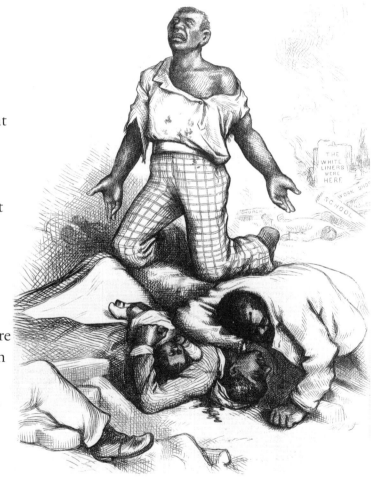

Some modern historians call the Ku Klux Klan trials a great victory. Through the judicial system and the presence of military troops, the federal government succeeded in breaking up the Klan, something that the Southern state governments had been unable or unwilling to do. These historians point to evidence that shows order returned to the chaotic South and that violence declined.

Other historians argue that the trials swept the dirt under the rug. White Northerners, they say, were more interested in suppressing rebellion than in truly protecting the lives and rights of Southern blacks. It's been estimated that tens of thousands of white men belonged to the Klan and that these men committed thousands of acts of violence against defenseless people.

A distraught man kneels by the victims of white violence. In the caption, artist Thomas Nast asks: "Is this a republican form of government? Is this protecting life, liberty, or property? Is this the equal protection of the laws?" *Harper's Weekly*, September 2, 1876; Library of Congress

Yet, despite the mass arrests, only 3,319 Klansmen were brought to trial in the Southern states; and of this number, only 1,143 resulted in conviction. Most of those convicted were simply fined or received light sentences or both. Others pleaded guilty in return for suspended sentences and a warning. The courts dropped the charges against the remaining 2,176 prisoners.

In May 1872, with the Ku Klux Klan trials over, Congress passed the Amnesty Act, pardoning most of the remaining Confederates, nearly 150,000. Only about 500 Rebels remained barred from voting or holding a political office.

That fall, President Grant ran for a second term and won easily. The next summer, he began to pardon those Klansmen serving sentences, saying the pardons were necessary in order to restore peace to a still chaotic South. The pardons allowed most Klansmen who had fled or gone into hiding to return home. Within four years, nearly all convicted Klansmen had either served out their sentences or had received pardons.

Despite these conciliatory moves, each state and local election brought a new wave of violence. New white supremacist groups flourished under different names such as the Rifle Clubs, the Red Shirts, the White League, the White Liners, and the White Caps. These groups intimidated black voters openly and violently.

Defying the Ku Klux Klan Act, some wore masks, as noted by a *Harper's Weekly* sketch artist: "Masked, armed, and supplied with horses and money by the Democratic candidates for office, they ride over the country at midnight, and perpetrate unheard-of enormities," wrote Thomas Nast. "They rob, they murder, they intimidate; yet no man, white or black, dares to denounce them."

By 1876, it had become evident that the public had grown tired of the decade-long crusade to reconstruct the South and protect the rights and lives of Southern blacks. Northern whites wanted a return to normalcy. They wanted peace and reunion with Southern whites.

That spring, the Supreme Court justices struck a blow to the Fourteenth and Fifteenth amendments when they pointed out

"The negroes of the South are free—
free as she'' says the parliamentary Wat-
terson. This is what the *State*, a well-
known Democratic organ of Tennessee,
says, in huge capitals, on the subject:
"Let it be known before the election that
the farmers have agreed to spot every
leading Radical negro in the county, and
treat him as an enemy for all time to come.
The rotten ring must and shall be broken
at any and all costs. The Democrats have
determined to withdraw all employment
from their enemies. Let this fact be
known."

inherent weaknesses in both amendments. Four years after the
Ku Klux Klan trials the Supreme Court ruled that the Fourteenth
Amendment did not give the federal government the power to act
against white supremacist groups and that the duty of protecting
citizens' equal rights "rests alone with the States."

In the fall of 1876, the presidential election proved too close
to declare a winner. After a bitter legal battle between Democrats
and Republicans, a compromise was reached in January 1877,
and Republican Rutherford B. Hayes was appointed president. As
president, Rutherford B. Hayes promised to leave the South alone.
Soon after taking office, he withdrew the last of the federal troops.
Reconstruction was over.

The famous abolitionist Frederick Douglass expressed the worry

In the days leading to the 1876 presidential election, many freedmen once again endured flagrant voter intimidation at the hands of Southern white supremacists.

Harper's Weekly, October 21, 1876; Special Collections, Binghamton University

of many black Americans. "If war among the whites brought peace and liberty to the blacks, what will peace among the whites bring?" he asked.

In the years after Reconstruction ended, Democrats continued to regain control throughout the South often through violent means. In state after state, they enacted new laws, called Jim Crow laws, that stripped away the political and civil rights of black Americans. The Jim Crow laws kept the lives of black Americans segregated and unequal in the South.

As the years passed, many white Americans grew nostalgic and sentimental about the years before the Civil War and the war itself. White Yankee and Rebel veterans began to participate together in Memorial Day observances, both in the North and the South. At these "reunions," the soldiers talked over old times, glorying in the battles and the soldier's life. Although roughly 179,000 black men had served as soldiers in the army and another 19,000 in the navy,

Former Yankee and Rebel soldiers shake hands in reconciliation at the 1913 Peace Jubilee, marking the fiftieth anniversary of the battle of Gettysburg. That year also marked the fiftieth anniversary of the Emancipation Proclamation. By 1913, most of the nation had embraced white supremacy and had sanctioned Jim Crow laws. That year alone, white mobs lynched fifty-one black Americans. Library of Congress

DEATH AT THE POLLS, AND FREE FROM "FEDERAL INTERFERENCE."

In this illustration called "Death at the Polls, and Free from Federal Interference," the artist Thomas Nast shows the consequences of the removal of federal troops from the South.

Harper's Weekly, October 18, 1879; Library of Congress

most were not invited to these gatherings and even told to stay away.

White authors and artists began to depict Southern life in ways that revised history, often portraying a romanticized view of plantation life and slavery. In novels, memoirs, and nonfiction books and articles, as well as mass-market magazines, Southern writers justified secession and the war, explained their defeat, venerated their leaders, and villianized the North. In popular culture and in their history, Southern writers created a literary and intellectual movement known as the Lost Cause, a belief that the Confederacy's cause was noble, its leaders chivalrous, and its military unmatched.

Some writers and historians glorified the Ku Klux Klan, creating a powerful mythology about the order and a distortion of history to justify its violence. In their work these writers continued to spread fear and false claims about "Negro domination," the freed people's unpreparedness for citizenship, their unwillingness to work and be

This engraving offers an idealized view of Southern life and race relations. By the early 1870s, such illustrations were becoming common, as white Americans struggled to put the war behind them and return to a sense of normalcy.

Harper's Weekly, December 30, 1871; Library of Congress

self-supporting, their propensity toward lawlessness and violence, and their incapacity to learn.

In 1905, white Americans clamored to read a best-selling romantic novel written by a Baptist minister. In *The Clansman,* Thomas Dixon portrayed the Klan as noble white-robed knights who burned crosses and saved white civilization from "Negro rule" and racial violence in the South. Dixon claimed the Klansmen were reluctant to take the law into their own hands and acted out of necessity.

In 1915, the producer D. W. Griffith transformed Dixon's racist novel into an epic silent motion picture, *The Birth of a Nation.* Despite protests by black Americans, the movie became a runaway box-office success.

Inspired by the movie, a group of white Southern men burned a cross on the top of Stone Mountain in Georgia. With this iconic first cross burning, the Ku Klux Klan was born again as a pro-Christian, pro-American brotherhood. This time, they added Catholics, Jews, immigrants, liberals, welfare recipients, and labor unions to their list of hates. Their membership swelled in the 1920s, including as many as five million men who dedicated themselves to white supremacy, conservative family values,

This illustration, called "The Fiery Cross of Old Scotland's Hills," comes from Thomas Dixon's 1905 novel, *The Clansman.* The Reconstruction-era Klansmen never practiced cross burning, but Dixon's novel would present fact as fiction and create a lasting myth about Reconstruction and the first Ku Klux Klan.

In 1925 Klansmen and women marched down Pennsylvania Avenue in Washington, D.C. It's estimated that nearly five million men and women belonged to the organization from all parts of the United States.

Library of Congress

and old-time religion. And yet, in the years that followed the Klan's rebirth, hate-driven lynch mobs—many of whom were known Klan members—would take the law into their own hands and murder at least 718 black men, women, and children, and eight white people.

In 1954, when the Supreme Court declared that the system of segregated schools in the United States was unconstitutional, Klan violence again surged in the South as black Americans enrolled in white schools and pushed to end segregation in other public areas as well. The Klan led brutal attacks on black men and women, who registered to vote or attempted to vote. They attacked men, women, and children who bravely crossed the color line to desegregate buses, theaters, diners, schools, and other public facilities.

Known Klansmen were responsible for the 1955 murder of Emmett Till, a fourteen-year-old boy who allegedly flirted or exchanged pleasantries with a white woman; the 1963 assassination of Medgar Evers, a black leader who organized a protest against still segregated schools in Jackson, Mississippi; the 1963 bombing of the Sixteenth Street Baptist Church that killed four black girls; the 1964 torture and murder of three young civil rights workers who registered voters in Mississippi; and the 1965 murder of a white civil rights worker named Viola Liuzzo.

During the 1960s, the Civil Rights movement would be viewed as the "Second Civil War," the "Second Reconstruction," and a "Second War of Northern Aggression." But ultimately the Ku Klux Klan and other white supremacists wouldn't win. Nearly one hundred years after the formation of the first Ku Klux Klan, the federal government passed the Civil Rights Act of 1964, banning discrimination in employment practices and public accommodations. The Voting Rights Act of 1965 restored and protected voting rights. In 1968, another Civil rights Act banned discrimination in the sale or rental of housing.

One year later, Congress passed the Federal Hate Crimes law, making it a federal offense for a person to willfully injure, intimidate, or interfere with another person's right to engage in federal protected activities such as voting, serving as a juror, attending school, patronizing a public place, or applying for employment on the basis of a person's race, color, religion, or national origin. Since then, the law has been broadened to include ethnicity, gender, sexual orientation, or disability, and covers crimes that involve threats, harassment, physical harm, or crimes against property motivated by prejudice.

Today, the Ku Klux Klan and other white supremacist groups continue to exist at the

The Knights of the Ku Klux Klan light a cross at their closing ceremony in 2006. The cross-lighting, they say, symbolizes the light of Christ, dispelling darkness and ignorance.

Photo taken by the author

fringes of the conservative right or as a separate political party altogether or with no political affiliation at all. In 2009 the Southern Poverty Law Center, located in Montgomery, Alabama, counted 932 active hate groups in the United States. The known activities of these groups range from murder and other acts of violence, intimidation, harassment, and vandalism, as well as speeches, meetings, and the spread of hate propaganda through leaflets, the Internet, and shortwave radio broadcasts.

Despite their numbers, these hate groups wield none of the power or prestige that the Ku Klux Klan held in earlier years. The Southern Poverty Law Center attributes their loss of power to Americans' intolerance of hate groups and their criminal activities and to law enforcement agencies who uphold our nation's laws. Modern historians also credit the large numbers of people who fight for real answers to social and economic problems and who fight for educational and economic opportunities for all Americans.

History is filled with stories of terrible things that happen as people stand up for an ideal and strike out against injustice. In 1857, before Emancipation and the Civil War, Frederick Douglass warned Americans that reform wouldn't be easy. "If there is no struggle, there is no progress," said Douglass. "Those who profess to favor freedom and yet depreciate agitation are men who want crops without plowing up the ground. They want rain without thunder and lightning. They want the ocean without the awful roar of its many waters."

Perhaps no one understood the difficulty of reform better than the freed people. Mittie Williams, the fourteen-year-old house slave who went fishing with her father the day the war ended, would never forget her father's excitement and the tug of his hand as he pulled her back to the Big House. In 1937, seventy-two years after the day the cannons boomed, Mittie Williams Freeman would remember that day and the years that followed as she recounted her life as a slave and a free woman. "It seem like it tuck a long time for freedom to come," she told her interviewer.

Indeed it did.

CIVIL RIGHTS TIME LINE

1863

- January. Lincoln issues Emancipation Proclamation, freeing all slaves living in the seceded Southern states.

1865

- February. General Sherman issues Special Field Order #15, which sets aside 400,000 acres in the Sea Islands region for exclusive settlement of the freed people, promising them forty-acre plots, mules, and possessory titles. President Johnson later vetoes the order and orders the freed people removed and the land returned to original owners.

- March. Freedmen's Bureau established.

- April. Civil War ends; Lincoln is assassinated.

- May. Andrew Johnson begins rapid and lenient presidential Reconstruction.

- June–August. Under Johnson's plan, the Southern state governments reorganize. Confederate leaders regain power.

- September. White Southern governments begin to pass restrictive Black Codes.

- December. Congress reconvenes and refuses to seat Southern representatives.

- December. Thirteenth Amendment ratified, abolishing slavery everywhere in the United States.

1866

- March. President Johnson vetoes bill to extend Freedmen's Bureau and Civil Rights Bill.

- April. Congress overrides Johnson's veto of Civil Rights Bill.

- May. Memphis riot. White civilians and police kill forty-six blacks and injure many more, burning ninety houses, twelve schools, and four churches.

- May. First Ku Klux Klan forms in Pulaski, Tennessee.

- June. Fourteenth Amendment proposed, entitling all persons born or naturalized in the United States to citizenship and equal protection under the laws of the United States.

- July. Congress passes new Freedmen's Bureau bill over Johnson's earlier veto, expanding the bureau's responsibilities and powers.

- July. Tennessee is readmitted to Union as first reconstructed state.

- July. Police in New Orleans storm a Republican meeting of blacks and whites on July 30, killing more than 40 and wounding more than 150.

- November. Republican election victories produce greater than two-thirds majorities in House and Senate.

- Most Southern states reject proposed Fourteenth Amendment.

1867

- March. Congress takes over Reconstruction from President Johnson and passes first Reconstruction Act, which divides South into five military districts, each under the command of a general. The act also guarantees freedmen the right to vote in elections for state constitutional conventions and in subsequent elections. Each Southern state is required to ratify the Fourteenth Amendment and its new constitution by majority vote, and then submit the constitution to Congress for approval.

- March. Second Reconstruction Act passes over Johnson's veto.

- April. Ku Klux Klan holds secret meeting to develop strategy to combat Republican plan for Reconstruction of the South and civil and political rights of black Americans.

- July. Third Reconstruction Act passes over Johnson's veto.

1868

- February. House impeaches Johnson.

- March. Fourth Reconstruction Act passes over Johnson's veto. The Second, Third, and Fourth acts provide details for voter registration boards, the adoption of new state constitutions, and the administration of "good faith" oaths on the part of white Southerners.

- May. Senate acquits Johnson by one vote.

- July. Seven more Southern states are readmitted to the Union under Radical plan: South Carolina, Florida, Alabama, Georgia, Louisiana, Arkansas, North Carolina.

- July. Fourteenth Amendment is ratified.

- September. Forrest claims that Klan membership numbers 550,000. Five days later, he recants estimate.

- September. The Opelousas Massacre in Louisiana leaves an estimated two hundred to three hundred black Americans dead.

- November. Former Union general Ulysses S. Grant (Republican) elected president. Black political leaders elected to state and local offices across the South.

- Sharecropping begins in parts of the South.

- Forrest orders Ku Klux Klan dens to disband after the presidential election.

1869

- February. Congress approves Fifteenth Amendment, which guarantees the vote to all male citizens regardless of color or previous condition of servitude.

- July. Freedmen's Bill expires. The Freedmen's Bureau continues its educational programs until 1872.

1870

- March. Congress passes Enforcement Act to enforce the Fourteenth Amendment. The act contains criminal penalties for those individuals who interfere with a citizen's right to vote.

- March. Congress ratifies the Fifteenth Amendment.

- U.S. Census reveals a white population of 39,818,449 and a black population of 4,880,009 (12 percent). Many white Southerners call the census "rigged," saying that it isn't possible for the freed people to thrive on their own.

1871

- April. Congress passes second Enforcement Act and Ku Klux Klan Act to further enforce the Fourteenth Amendment, making it a federal offense to abrogate an individual's civil and political rights. The act also provides for election supervisors and permits martial law and the suspension of the writ of habeas corpus to combat murders, beatings, and threats by the Klan.

- May–December. Ku Klux Klan trials take place in Southern states.

1872

- May. Grant issues Amnesty Act, pardoning most of remaining Rebels. Only five hundred former Confederates remain barred from holding political office.

- Summer. Freedmen's Bureau discontinues educational programs.

- November. Grant is reelected. He begins to pardon convicted Klansmen.

- In elections, Democrats regain control of four state governments by 1872.

1873

- April. After a disputed election in Colfax, Louisiana, well-armed whites attack blacks, killing fifty blacks and three whites.

1874

- Democrats win majority in the House of Representatives.

1875

- Several Grant appointees indicted for corruption.

- March. Congress passes Civil Rights Act of 1875, granting equal rights in public accommodations such as inns and theaters, in transportation, and while serving jury duty.

- September. Armed whites kill thirty black church leaders and teachers, and white Republican officials in Clinton, Mississippi.

1876

- Supreme Court weakens Reconstruction-era amendments by emasculating the enforcement clause of the Fourteenth Amendment and revealing deficiencies in the Fifteenth Amendment.

- Summer. Race riots and terrorism directed at blacks occur in South Carolina. President Grant sends federal troops to restore order.

- November. The outcome in the Electoral College proves too close to call in the presidential election of Samuel Tilden (Democrat) versus Rutherford B. Hayes (Republican).

- Democratic Party regains control of four more (total of eight) state governments by 1876.

1877

- January. After much negotiation, Southern Democratic leaders agree to appoint Rutherford B. Hayes (Republican) president. Hayes orders withdrawal of federal troops from the South.

- "Home rule" returns to South Carolina, Louisiana, and Florida, the only three Southern states not yet controlled by Democrats. Home rule allows these states to determine their own government structure.

1883

- Supreme Court invalidates 1875 Civil Rights Act, ruling that the federal government cannot bar discrimination by corporations or individuals.

1896

- Supreme Court approves "separate but equal" segregation doctrine.

1915

- Rebirth of the Ku Klux Klan in Georgia.

1923

- Oklahoma placed under martial law because of Ku Klux Klan activities.

1925

- Ku Klux Klan marches on Washington. The *New York Times* estimates 50,000 to 60,000 Klansmen and women. Others estimate as many as 200,000.

1954

- U.S. Supreme Court declares school segregation unconstitutional in *Brown v. Board of Education of Topeka* ruling.

1955

- Rosa Parks refuses to move to the back of a Montgomery, Alabama, bus as required by a city ordinance; boycott follows and bus segregation ordinance is declared unconstitutional.

- Fourteen-year-old Emmett Till is brutally murdered in Mississippi. Two white men, J. W. Milam and Roy Bryant, are acquitted. The two men later admit that they killed Till.

1957

- Arkansas governor Orval Faubus deploys National Guard to block nine black students from attending a Little Rock High School; following a court order, President Eisenhower sends in federal troops to ensure compliance.

1960

- Four black college students begin sit-ins at lunch counter of a Greensboro, North Carolina, restaurant where black patrons are not served.

- Ruby Bridges, age six, is the first African American child to attend an all-white school in the South.

1961

- Freedom Rides begin from Washington, D.C., into the segregated Southern states in an effort to test the Supreme Court's decision to outlaw racial segregation in the restaurants and waiting rooms in terminals that serve buses crossing state lines.

1962

- President Kennedy sends federal troops to the University of Mississippi to quell riots so that James Meredith, the school's first black student, can attend.

- The Supreme Court rules that segregation is unconstitutional in all transportation facilities.

1963

- Civil rights leader Medgar Evers is killed by a sniper's bullet. In 1994, Klansman Byron De La Beckwith is convicted of the murder.

- Dr. Martin Luther King Jr. delivers "I Have a Dream" speech to hundreds of thousands during the March on Washington.

- Church bombing in Birmingham, Alabama, leaves four young black girls dead and injures twenty. In 1977, known Klansman Robert Chambliss is found guilty of first-degree murder and sentenced to life in prison. In 2001 and 2002, two more Klansmen, Thomas Blanton Jr. and Bobby Frank Cherry, are also found guilty of first-degree murder and sentenced to life in prison.

1964

- Congress passes Civil Rights Act declaring discrimination based on race illegal, after seventy-five-day long filibuster.

- Three civil rights workers disappear in Mississippi after being stopped for speeding; found buried six weeks later. In 2005, Edgar Ray Killen was convicted of three counts of manslaughter and sentenced to sixty years in prison. Killen, a segregationist, organized the Klansmen who killed the workers.

1965

- March. Six hundred activists march from Selma to Montgomery, Alabama, to demand protection for voting rights.

- New voting rights act signed.

1966

- Edward Brooke (R-Massachusetts) elected first black U.S. senator in eighty-five years.

1967

- Riots in Detroit, Newark, New Jersey.

- Thurgood Marshall becomes first African American to be named to the Supreme Court.

- Carl Stokes (Cleveland) and Richard G. Hatcher (Gary, Indiana) are elected first black mayors of major U.S. cities.

1968

- Martin Luther King Jr. is assassinated in Memphis, Tennessee; James Earl Ray is later convicted and sentenced to ninety-nine years in prison.

1969

- Congress passes a Federal Hate Crimes Law, making it a federal offense for a person to willingly injure, intimidate, or interfere with another person's attempt to engage in federally protected activities on the basis of the victim's color, race, religion, or national origin. In 1994, an enforcement act broadens the law to include ethnicity and gender. In 2008, the law is broadened to include sexual orientation, gender identity, or disability, and dropped the prerequisite that the victim be engaging in a federally protected activity.

1973

- Maynard Jackson (Atlanta) is elected first black mayor of a major Southern U.S. city.

1975

- Voting Rights Act extended.

1979

- Shoot-out in Greensboro, North Carolina, leaves five anti-Klan protesters dead; twelve Klansmen are charged with murder.

1983

- Martin Luther King Jr. federal holiday is established.

1988

- Congress passes Civil Rights Restoration Act over President Reagan's veto.

1989

- Army General Colin Powell becomes first African American to serve as chairman of the Joint Chiefs of Staff.
- L. Douglas Wilder (Virginia) becomes first African American elected governor.

1990

- President George H.W. Bush vetoes a civil rights bill he says would impose quotas for employers; weaker bill passes in 1991.

1996

- Supreme Court rules consideration of race in creating congressional districts is unconstitutional.

2008

- Barack Obama elected first African American president of the United States.

President Barack Obama
Official White House Photo by Pete Souza

QUOTE ATTRIBUTIONS

"The method of force . . ."
W. E. B. Du Bois, *Black Reconstruction in America, 1860–1880* (New York: Atheneum, [1935] 1975), 677–78.

1. *"Bottom Rail Top"*

"She skeered to stay by herself." Mittie (Williams) Freeman, Slave Narratives, Arkansas, vol. 2, part 2, 347.

"slavery stands in the way . . ." Joseph T. Glathaar, *The March to the Sea and Beyond: Sherman's Troops in the Savannah and Carolinas Campaign* (Baton Rouge: Louisiana State University Press, 1995), 41.

"I never in my life . . ." Abraham Lincoln, as quoted in Doris Kearns Goodwin, *Team of Rivals: The Political Genius of Abraham Lincoln* (New York: Simon and Schuster, 2005), 499.

"We heard that lots of slaves . . ." Freeman, 348.

"Pappy jumps up . . ." Freeman, 348.

"Such equality does not in fact exist . . ." Edward McPherson, LL.D., *The Political History of the United States During the Period of Reconstruction*, 2nd edition (Washington, D.C.: Solomons and Chapman, 1876), 474–75.

"If they don't belong . . ." Myrta Avary, *Dixie After the War* (New York: Doubleday, Page and Co., 1906), 152.

" 'Course she is our nigger . . ." Delicia Patterson, Slave Narratives, Missouri, vol. 10, 273.

"We had all our earnings . . ." Victoria Clayton, *Black and White Under the Old Regime* (Milwaukee, Wis.: Young Churchman Co., 1899), 167–68.

"We came out of the war . . ." Samuel Gholson, KKK Report, Mississippi, vol. 2, 852.

"Hello, massa . . ." *New York Times*, August 17, 1865, 1.

"My father kept pointing out . . ." Martin Jackson, Slave Narratives, Texas, vol. 14, part 2, 189.

"With malice toward none . . ." Abraham Lincoln, Second Inaugural Address, March 4, 1865 (Abraham Lincoln Papers, Library of Congress, series 3, General Correspondence, 1837–1897, www.loc.gov).

"I 'lect Uncle Charlie Burns . . ." Sarah Ford, Slave Narratives, Texas, vol. 16, part 2, 45–46.

2. *"Boys, Let Us Get Up a Club"*

"We could not engage . . ." John Lester and D. L. Wilson, *Ku Klux Klan: Its Origin, Growth, and Disbandment* (New York: Da Capo Press, [1905] 1973), 52, 59.

"operated in favor . . ." Andrew Johnson, as quoted in Eric Foner, *Reconstruction: America's Unfinished Revolution, 1863–1877* (New York: HarperCollins, 1988), 250.

"When people abroad condemn . . ." *Pulaski Citizen*, May 11, 1866, 2.

"During the evening the wildest . . ." *Harper's Weekly*, May 26, 1866, 1.

"Boys, let us get . . ." Lester and Wilson, 53.

"Call it *ku klux* . . ." Lester and Wilson, 54.

"There was a weird potency . . ." Lester and Wilson, 54.

"There may be in their conduct . . ." Lester and Wilson, 127.

3. *"I Was Killed at Chickamauga"*

"A dreary desolate . . ." Lester and Wilson, 61.

"It was a pretty . . ." Daniel Coleman, KKK Report, Alabama, vol. 2, 660.

"Its mysteriousness was . . ." Lester and Wilson, 68.

"Take notice . . ." *Pulaski Citizen*, March 29, 1867, 3.

"Will any one venture . . ." *Pulaski Citizen*, March 29, 1867, 3.

"Place him before the royal altar . . ." Lester and Wilson, 63.

"O wad some power . . ." Robert L. Stevenson, as quoted in Lester and Wilson, 63.

"The den rang with shouts . . ." Lester and Wilson, 64.

"A spirit from the other world . . ." Lester and Wilson, 73.

"In this way, the Klan . . ." Lester and Wilson, 74.

"Dem Ku Klux just come . . ." Ann Ulrich Evans, Slave Narratives, Missouri, vol. 10, 116.

"The reason I was scared . . ." Reuben Sheets, KKK Report, Georgia, vol. 2, 651.

"a band of regulators" Lester and Wilson, 75.

"It will increase the government . . ." *Pulaski Citizen*, February 9, 1866, 3.

"I do not think . . ." Nathan Bedford Forrest, KKK Report, Florida and Miscellaneous, vol. 13, 34.

"They considered that good faith . . ." Robert Aldrich, KKK Report, South Carolina, vol. 1, 171.

"It is hoped . . ." Nathan Bedford Forrest, *Official Records of the Union and Confederate Armies*, series 1, vol. 32, part 1 (Washington D.C.: Government Printing Office), 610.

"The incorrigibles still indulge . . ." Carl S. Schurz, *Report on the Conditions of the South*, December 19, 1865, 39th Congress, 1st session. (Bibliobazaar, 2006), 14–15.

"Those whose intellects are . . ." Schurz, 14–15.

"Our visitor appeared . . ." *Pulaski Citizen*, April 19, 1867, 3.

"Time will fully develop . . ." *Pulaski Citizen*, April 19, 1867, 3.

"On last Wednesday night . . ." *Pulaski Citizen*, April 19, 1867, 3.

"First time dey come . . ." Lorenza Ezell, Slave Narratives, Texas, vol. 16, part 2, 30.

4. *"Worms Would Have Been Eating Me Now"*

"We the * * [Ku Klux] . . ." Lester and Wilson, 154.

"The Klan Leaders desired on one hand . . ." Lester and Wilson, 90.

"We chose General Forrest." James R. Crowe, as quoted in Brian Steel Wills, *A Battle from the Start: The Life of Nathan Bedford Forrest* (New York: HarperCollins, 1992), 336.

"incapable alike . . ." *New York Times*, October 30, 1877, 1.

"There was a great deal . . ." Forrest, 6–7.

"They admitted no man . . ." Forrest, 22.

"Pretty nigh everybody . . ." W. P. Burnett, KKK Report, South Carolina, vol. 3, 1985–86.

"It was thought . . ." Coleman, 661.

"in caves in the bowels . . ." James M. Beard, *K.K.K. Sketches* (Philadelphia: Claxton, Remsen, Haffellfinger, 1877), 72–73.

"Wherever a petty tyrant . . ." As reprinted in the *Zion's Herald*, April 23, 1868, 45, 17.

"The Sergeant and Scorpion . . ." Avary, 269.

"The Death Watch . . ." Avary, 269.

"Burst your cerements . . ." Avary, 269.

"The very night of the day . . ." Ryland Randolph, as quoted in Lester and Wilson, 41–42.

"[They] told me that . . ." Jacob Davis, *The Ku Klux Klan in Middle and West Tennessee*, September 2, 1868, 32.

"Have you a pin?" John Harrill, KKK Report, North Carolina, 208.

"The Ku Klux did not consider . . ." Ryland Randolph, as quoted in Stanley F. Horn, *Invisible Empire: The Story of the Ku Klux Klan, 1866–1871* (Cos Cob, Conn.: John E. Edwards, 1969), 45–46.

"What is called a raid . . ." James Justice, KKK Report, North Carolina, 136.

"Is he fat?" Samuel Horton, KKK Report, Alabama, vol. 2, 729–32.

"We were to swear . . ." John Harrill, KKK Report, North Carolina, 205.

"We were to obey . . ." James Grant, KKK Report, North Carolina, 231.

"I did not believe . . ." Grant, 232.

"My neighbors told me   " William Jolly, KKK Report, South Carolina, vol. 3, 1972.

"They told me I had better . . ." Christenberry Tait, KKK Report, South Carolina, vol. 3, 1974.

"I was pressed . . ." Junius Tyndall, KKK Report, South Carolina, vol. 3, 1988.

"There was no way . . ." William Owens, KKK Report, South Carolina, vol. 3, 1396.

"The slave went free . . ." W. E. B. Du Bois, *Black Reconstruction in America, 1860–1880* (New York: Atheneum, [1935] 1975), 30.

"These human beings . . ." Du Bois, 677–78.

"I loved the old government . . ." Forrest, 33.

5. *"They Say a Man Ought Not to Vote"*

"Your days are numbered . . ." "A Memento of Reconstruction," *Cleveland Gazette*, February 8, 1890, 1.

"I do believe it . . ." Elias Hill, KKK Report, South Carolina, vol. 3, 1412.

"endeavor to administer . . ." Edward McPherson, *The Political History of the United States of America During the Period of Reconstruction* (Washington D.C.: James Chapman, 1880), 365–66.

"The laws of this State . . ." Charles H. Pearce, KKK Report, Florida and Miscellaneous, 165–66.

"He handed one to me . . ." Burton Long, KKK Report, Alabama, vol. 2, 1149–50.

"Mister, you can't call . . ." Long, 1150.

"I do not think . . ." Augustus Wright, KKK Report, Georgia, vol. 1, 93.

"Realizing that the vote . . ." Isaiah Green, Slave Narratives, Georgia, vol. 4, part 2, 55.

"We call them enemies . . ." Robert Gleed, KKK Report, Mississippi, vol. 2, 725.

"[They] have dishonored . . ." As quoted in James McPherson, *Ordeal by Fire: The Civil War and Reconstruction* (New York: McGraw Hill, 2000), 557.

"the meanest, most detestable . . ." Letter written by Milus S. Carroll in 1924, Manuscript Collection, York County Historical Society, South Carolina.

"My political crime is . . ." William Wyatt, *The Ku Klux Klan in Middle and West Tennessee* (September 2, 1868), 17.

"They whipped me very hard . . ." Charles Belefont, *The Ku Klux Klan in Middle and West Tennessee*, 23.

"I have no powder . . ." Forrest, 34.

"My daddy charge with . . ." Lorenza Ezell, Slave Narratives, Texas, vol. 16, 30.

"If we are to be . . ." *New York Times*, September 8, 1868, 1.

"A man can kill . . ." Henry Lipscomb, KKK Report, South Carolina, vol. 2, 683.

"The white people of our state . . ." Walter Fleming, ed., *Documentary History of Reconstruction*, vol. 1 (Cleveland, Ohio: The Arthur H. Clark Co., 1907), 455–56.

"As soon as they found . . ." Henry Johnson, KKK Report, South Carolina, vol. 1, 324.

"They say a man . . ." Robert Meacham, KKK Report, Florida and Miscellaneous, 102.

"an institution of Chivalry . . . laws of the land" Lester and Wilson, 88.

"Have you ever been rejected . . ." Prescript, Lester and Wilson, 171–72.

"I was trying . . ." Forrest, 8.

"We was a-sitting . . ." Gabe Hines, Slave Narratives, Alabama, vol. 1, 179.

6. *"I Am Going to Die on This Land"*

"I worked night and day . . ." George Taylor, KKK Report, Alabama, vol. 1, 575.

"A gentleman who commits . . ." John Schofield, *Harper's Weekly*, March 23, 1867, 184.

"In the months of August . . ." Robert Meacham, KKK Report, Florida and Miscellaneous, 101.

"Old marse said . . ." Fred James, Slave Narratives, South Carolina, vol. 14, part 3, 15.

"They listened to every sort . . ." P. T. Sayre, KKK Report, Alabama, vol. 1, 357.

"He was as fine a man . . ." George Taylor, KKK Report, Alabama, vol. 1, 574.

"I had a bargain . . ." Taylor, 573.

"just out of the moon" Taylor, 574.

"My losses . . ." Taylor, 573.

"I worked and labored hard . . ." Taylor, 574.

"If they find a Negro . . ." W. L. Bost, Slave Narratives, North Carolina, vol. 11, part 1, 144.

"The running off . . ." George Garner, KKK Report, South Carolina, vol. 1, 397.

"I tell you this [kukluxism] . . ." Mack Tinker, KKK Report, Alabama, vol. 2, 1362–63.

"They told him that darkeys . . ." Allen P. Huggins, KKK Report, Mississippi, vol. 1, 277–78.

"They did not intend . . ." John Tayloe Coleman, KKK Report, Alabama, vol. 2, 1051.

"There is no intention . . ." Joseph W. Gelray, *Report of the Secretary of War* (Washington, D.C.: Government Printing Office, 1868), 181.

"They beat my breath . . ." Doc Roundtree, KKK Report, Florida and Miscellaneous, 279.

"I am going to die . . ." Hannah Tutson, KKK Report, Florida and Miscellaneous, 61.

"You can tell your old man . . ." Tutson, 62.

"In the red times . . ." Tutson, 60.

"I had been working . . ." Tutson, 60.

"They whipped me . . ." Tutson, 60.

"I told them to . . ." Tutson, 61.

"My little daughter . . ." Tutson, 61.

"Negroes had to go to school . . ." Jefferson Franklin Henry, Slave Narratives, Georgia, vol. 4, part 2, 191.

7. "A Whole Race Trying to Go to School"

"I was inclined . . ." Cornelius McBride, KKK Report, Mississippi, vol. 1, 333.

"I went to school . . ." Sarah Frances Shaw Graves, Slave Narratives, Missouri, vol. 10, 135, 136.

"The schools are firmly . . ." *Harper's Weekly,* May 25, 1867.

"We should teach . . ." Avary, 320.

"Every little negro . . ." Letter from A. W. Moore to E. H. Dabbs, April 30, 1870, as quoted in Leon F. Litwack, *Been in the Storm So Long: The Aftermath of Slavery* (New York: Vintage Books, 1980), 489.

"The piling up . . ." "The Ku Klux Movement," *Atlantic Monthly* 87, no. 523 (May 1901), 635–36.

"We have nothing . . ." *American Missionary* 12, no. 3 (March 1868), 60.

"If the freedmen . . ." Schurz, 50.

"If we have social equality . . ." David Macrae, *The Americans at Home: Pen-and-Ink Sketches of American Men, Manners, and Institutions,* vol. 2 (Edinburgh, Scotland: Emerson and Douglas, 1870), 19.

"Whenever it is written . . ." Booker T. Washington, *Up from Slavery: An Autobiography* (New York: Doubleday, Page, and Co., 1919), 58, 62.

"That was the only place . . ." Oscar Judkins, KKK Report, Alabama, vol. 3, 1043, 1047.

"There is the man . . ." William H. Forney, KKK Report, Alabama, vol. 1, 470.

"Could not be whipped . . ." Joseph Speed, KKK Report, Alabama, vol. 1, 429.

"I know I've done . . ." William Luke, as quoted in Gene L. Howard, *Death at Cross Plains: An Alabama Reconstruction Tragedy* (Tuscaloosa: University of Alabama Press, 1984), 90.

"My Dear Wife . . ." William C. Luke, U.S. Congress, *Congressional Globe,* 42nd Congress, 1st session (1871), 477.

"They took every book . . ." Caroline Smith, KKK Report, Georgia, vol. 1, 401.

"All its flaming tail. . ." *Tuskaloosa Independent Monitor,* September 21, 1869, 2.

"When I gather my posse . . ." John Minnis, KKK Report, Alabama, vol. 1, 559.

"1st quarter, 8th Bloody moon . . ." *American Missionary* 12, no. 8 (August 12, 1868), 183.

"I did not pay . . ." Cornelius McBride, KKK Report, Mississippi, vol. 1, 329.

"You God damned Yankee . . ." McBride, 326.

"Shooting is too good . . ." McBride, 327.

"They swore terribly . . ." McBride, 327.

"The blood was running . . ." McBride, 329.

"It was a whole race . . ." Washington, 30.

"The strongest chains . . ." as quoted in Gladys-Marie Fry, *Night Riders in Black Folk History* (Chapel Hill: University of North Carolina, 2001), 41.

"Our white folks . . ." Susan Merritt, *Slave Narratives,* Texas, vol. 16, part 3, 77.

8. "They Need Somebody to Guide Them"

"It is impossible to separate . . ." Charles H. Pearce, KKK Report, Florida and Miscellaneous, 171.

"De colored preachers . . ." Mack Taylor, Slave Narratives, South Carolina, vol. 14, part 4, 159.

"You are not to preach . . ." Dennis Rice, KKK Report, vol. 2, 1182.

"When they have confined . . ." H. D. D. Twiggs, KKK Report, Georgia, vol. 2, 1055–56.

"The preacher made frequent . . ." *New Orleans Tribune,* September 9, 1865, 1.

"Some of them said . . ." James Grant, KKK Report, North Carolina, 235–36.

"Nearly every colored church . . ." William Dougherty, KKK Report, Alabama, vol. 2, 1025.

"There was scarcely a night . . ." Carroll, letter, 2.

"Headquarters K.K.K." *Columbia (South Carolina) Daily Phoenix,* February 1, 1871, 1.

"I thought my pitiful condition . . ." Hill, 1411.

"Haven't you been preaching . . ." Hill, 1407.

"Don't pray against us . . ." Hill, 1408.

"Those whites that professed . . ." Hill, 1411.

"I don't preach political sermons . . ." R. E. Cooper, KKK Report, South Carolina, vol. 3, 1956–57.

"We proudly point . . ." A. B. Osgood, KKK Report, Florida and Miscellaneous, 171.

9. *"Forced by Force, to Use Force"*

"They insulted white people . . ." William Simpson, KKK Report, South Carolina, vol. 3, 1304.

"Theire is great excitement . . ." Mary Davis Brown diaries, January 30, 1871, film book 0299, reel 3, Special Collections, Ellis Library, University of Missouri.

"Folks were pretty much scared . . ." James Long, KKK Report, South Carolina, vol. 3, 1764.

"kill from the cradle up . . ." See KKK Report, South Carolina, vol. 3, 1758–60, 1763–65, 1781–89, 1797, 1809, 1815, 1817, 1835, 1900.

"He always felt at liberty . . ." Julia Rainey, KKK Report, South Carolina, vol. 3, 1750.

"He and his company . . ." Carroll, letter, 4.

"I was scared . . ." Rosy Williams, KKK Report, South Carolina, vol. 3, 1721.

"He died cursing . . ." Carroll, letter, 8.

"The intelligent, honest white people . . ." *Yorkville Enquirer*, March 9, 1871, as quoted in KKK Report, South Carolina, vol. 3, 1347–48.

"It requires great patience . . ." Lewis Merrill, May 19, 1871. RG 393, part 5, Post of Yorkville, SC, entry 1, letters sent, vol. 1, 22. National Archives.

"That the power to correct . . ." Grant to Congress, *KKK Conspiracy*, 1.

"White men would be arrested . . ." Avary, 276.

"If the Federal Government . . ." Benjamin Butler, *Congressional Globe*, House of Representatives, 42nd Congress, 1st session, April 4, 1871, 448.

"And I want to say . . ." Carroll, letter, 3.

10. *"The Sacredness of the Human Person"*

"Isn't one of you gentlemen . . ." Samuel Tutson, KKK Report, Florida, 59.

"They are afraid to stay . . ." Daniel Lipscomb, KKK Report, South Carolina, vol. 1, 430, 432.

"We do not believe . . ." Hill, 1410, 1412, 1415.

"I was the only one . . ." McBride, 331.

"As a general thing . . ." McBride, 339.

"Luke had made himself . . ." Peter Dox, KKK Report, Alabama, vol. 1, 429.

"I think this organization . . ." Forrest, 7.

"The whole statement is wrong . . ." Forrest, 4.

"information from others" Forrest, 6.

"I talked with different people . . ." Forrest, 12.

"I've been lying . . ." As quoted in Horn, 316.

"deplorable ignorance" Judge Hugh Bond, KKK Report, South Carolina, vol. 3, 1983.

"I know I done wrong . . ." William Self, KKK Report, South Carolina, vol. 3, 1988.

"unmanly" Bond, 1988.

"Would you not have thought?" Bond, 1974–75.

"None of you seems to have . . ." Bond, 1983.

"They cannot exist together . . ." Bond, 1984.

"Every man has to . . ." Jackson, 189.

Epilogue. *"It Tuck a Long Time"*

"Masked, armed, and supplied . . ." *Harper's Weekly*, October 24, 1874, 878.

"If war among the whites . . ." Frederick Douglass, as quoted in David W. Blight, *Race and Reunion: The Civil War in American Memory* (Cambridge, Mass.: Belknap Press of Harvard University Press, 2002), 131.

"If there is no struggle . . ." Frederick Douglass, speech given at Canandaigua, New York.

"It seem like it tuck . . ." Freeman, 348.

This highway rolls through the picturesque countryside as it leads into Pulaski, Tennessee.

Photograph by the author

BIBLIOGRAPHY AND SOURCE NOTES

Travel informs my work, and I like to visit the places I write about. One of the places I visited was Pulaski, Tennessee.

As my husband and I rode along Highway 31A that leads into the town, I gazed out the passenger window at the rolling countryside and imagined nightriders thundering under a bright moon, their white robes billowing like wings. I imagined the sound of the horses' hooves as the riders pounded their way toward a small, dark cabin belonging to a freedman who had dared to vote or exercise his freedom in other ways. The sounds of a whipping, I knew, were known to carry a mile or more. It is natural and human to respond when you hear a cry of distress, and I imagined his neighbors, too terrified to help.

We continued into Pulaski, and just off the picturesque town square, we parked across the street from the low white brick building where more than 140 years earlier, six returning Confederate soldiers had lounged each evening in the months that followed surrender and where John Lester said, "Boys, let us get up a club."

Nearly fifty years later, in 1916, the Daughters of the Confederacy mounted a bronze plaque on the building, commemorating the Klan's birth and its six founders, and there it stayed for nearly seventy years. In the early 1990s, after the building changed hands, its new owner reversed the bronze plaque so that only its smooth, green weathered surface shows to passersby.

Still, I wanted a photograph, and as I lifted my camera, an older woman walked past and said, "You thinking of writing a story about that backwards-turned plaque?"

"It's an interesting story, isn't it?" I said.

This present day photograph shows the law office where the six Pulaski men lounged in 1866. A bronze plaque commemorating the six men can be seen, turned backwards, here.

Photograph by the author

"We're about sick of it around here," she said crisply, and continued across the street.

And so the town of Pulaski is. Pulaski doesn't ignore its past. In fact, the quaint and friendly Southern town is proud of its role in American history, but its residents disavowed the Klan many years ago. Although Klan members from other states continue to flock to Pulaski to hold "White Heritage Festivals," the primarily white town repudiates the Klan. The backwards-turned plaque symbolizes that repudiation.

Still, as I walked the Pulaski streets that day, I thought about that plaque and the countless memorials to Confederate war heroes such as Nathan Bedford Forrest that I had seen on this trip and other trips to the South, and I thought about the question that had launched this book during another trip several years earlier: What about the thousands of victims of Klan violence? Where are their memorials?

It was that question that had prompted me to call the Southern Poverty Law Center in Montgomery, Alabama, an organization internationally known for its tolerance education programs, its legal victories against white supremacists, and its tracking of hate groups.

I asked if anyone at the center could tell me if any plaques, markers, or statues commemorate the lives of the victims of Klan violence during the Reconstruction years.

I was told there are none.

The sources noted here are intended to refer interested readers to more detailed historical works and to provide helpful information on the various works consulted in the research and writing of this book.

For thorough and up-to-date scholarship that compellingly refutes long-standing misconceptions of Reconstruction, I relied on Eric Foner's *Reconstruction: America's Unfinished Revolution, 1863–1877* (New York: Harper and Row, 1988) and his *Forever Free: The Story of Emancipation and Reconstruction* (New York: Vintage Books, 2006). These two books offer new perspectives and information about the black experience during Reconstruction as well as the role of the Freedmen's Bureau and its agents, "carpetbaggers," Republicans, teachers, and preachers. In the latter book, *Forever Free,* I found illuminating Joshua Brown's visual essays and commentary about contemporaneous images and their influence on the reading public. James M. McPherson's *Ordeal by Fire: The Civil War and Reconstruction* (New York: McGraw Hill, 2000)

This large tribute to Nathan Bedford Forrest stands on private property outside Nashville, Tennessee.

Photograph by the author

also proved a useful source, especially for its economic and political discussions.

Leon Litwack's *Been in the Storm So Long: The Aftermath of Slavery* (New York: Vintage Books, 1979) offered a rich look at the way that blacks and whites shaped Southern history in the areas of emancipation, education, and religion during Reconstruction; W. E. B. Du Bois's *Black Reconstruction in America, 1860–1880* (New York: Atheneum, 1975, 1935) offered a vital discussion on the role of African Americans in labor and economics. Jane Turner Censer's *The Reconstruction of White Southern Womanhood, 1865–1895* (Baton Rouge: University of Louisiana Press, 2003) offered a new perspective on elite white Southern women, arguing that "southern belles" forged self-reliant and independent identities that challenged the "helpless" stereotype wrought in popular culture and exploited by the Klan.

Other essential scholarly texts include David W. Blight's *Race and Reunion* (Cambridge, Mass.: Belknap Press of Harvard University Press, 2002) and *Beyond the Battlefield: Race, Memory, and the American War* (Amherst: University of Massachusetts Press, 2002). One of the foremost scholars in the area of cultural memory, Blight discusses white Southerners' use of propaganda to shape and spin perceptions of the Civil War and Reconstruction into a mythic "Lost Cause" that lives on today, especially in racist subcultures. He also reminds us that great violence has been committed in the name of memory.

Gladys-Marie Fry's classic *Night Riders in Black Folk History* (Knoxville: University of Tennessee Press, 1975) is also essential reading. This work follows the nightrider through folklore and oral history for an especially compelling study of antebellum patrollers and the postwar Klan's manipulation of blacks through terror and intimidation.

Histories on the Ku Klux Klan tend to fall into two broad groups: well-documented texts written by trained historians and those largely undocumented or poorly documented texts written by others. For serious scholarship, I recommend David M. Chalmers's *Hooded Americanism: The History of the Ku Klux Klan* (Durham, N.C.: Duke University Press, 1987), Allen W. Trelease's *White Terror: The Ku Klux Klan Conspiracy and Southern Reconstruction* (Baton Rouge: Louisiana State University Press, 1971), and Wyn Craig Wade's *The Fiery Cross: The Ku Klux Klan in America* (New York: Simon and Schuster, 1987).

Also essential is Herbert Shapiro's *White Violence and Black Response: From Reconstruction to Montgomery* (Amherst: University of Massachusetts Press, 1988). Shapiro argues that a society committed to racism cannot be maintained without violence. He traces the violent reactions of white supremacists as African Americans moved toward genuine equality. Kwando M. Kinshasa's *Black Resistance to the Ku Klux Klan in the Wake of the Civil War* (Jefferson, N.C.: McFarland and Company, 2006) was also helpful.

Other insightful sources include J. Michael Martinez's *Carpetbaggers, Cavalry, and the Ku Klux Klan: Exposing the Invisible Empire During Reconstruction* (Lanham, Md.: Rowman and Littlefield Publishers, 2007) and Nancy MacLean's *Behind the Mask of Chivalry: The Making of the Second Ku Klux Klan* (New York: Oxford University Press, 1994). Although she focuses on the second era of the Klan, MacLean's scholarship was especially helpful in understanding how extremist groups developed in the United States and in Germany during the 1920s, with very different results.

An older text that for the most part has stood the test of time is William Peirce Randel's *The Ku Klux Klan: A Century of Infamy* (Philadelphia: Chilton Company, 1965). Elaine Franz Parsons's 2005 article "Midnight Rangers: Costumes and Performances in the Reconstruction-Era Ku Klux Klan," found in the *Journal of American History* (vol. 92, no. 3, pp. 811–35), offers an interesting look at the Klansmen's macabre theatrics during their brutal raids.

I also consulted with white supremacist perspectives on the Klan and Reconstruction written by Klan apologists. These include Colonel Winfield Jones's *Story of the Ku Klux Klan* (Washington, D.C.: American Newspaper Syndicate, 1921) and Stanley Horn's *Invisible Empire: The Story of the Ku Klux Klan, 1866–1871* (Cos Cob, Conn.: John E. Edwards, 1969). These biased accounts are noteworthy for their contribution to a legacy of deformed understandings of the Ku Klux Klan and its role during Reconstruction.

Primary evidence about the Klan's formation is fragmentary at best, mostly coming from an account titled *Ku Klux Klan, Its Origins, Growth, and Disbandment.* Published in 1884 by founding member John Lester and coauthor D. L. Wilson, this so-called history lacks detail, and many details, where present, are inaccurate.

Scholars such as David Blight remind us of the power of memory to turn history into myth and, I add, myth into history.

Interpretation often depends upon the lens through which we view history. It should be noted that Lester's account was written at a time when many white Southerners constructed their own versions of the past in memoirs and histories. In their writings, they vindicated Southern secession, glorified the Confederate soldier, and rationalized the Klan's violence during Reconstruction. Works such as these helped to forge and propagate the Lost Cause tradition. Other "Lost Cause" writings consulted for this book include Victoria V. Clayton's *White and Black Under the Old Regime* (Milwaukee, Wisc.: the Young Churchman, 1899) and Myrta Lockett Avary's *Dixie After the War* (New York: Doubleday, 1906), among others.

For a contrasting firsthand view of the South after the war, readers should refer to Carl Schurz's *Report on the Condition of the South* (1865), reprinted by Bibliobazaar; and Albion Winegar Tourgée's *The Invisible Empire* (1880), reprinted by the Louisiana State University Press in 1989.

Today, Nathan Bedford Forrest remains an enigma. For more information I recommend Paul Ashdown and Edward Caudill's *The Myth of Nathan Bedford Forrest* (Lanham, Md: Rowman and Littlefield Publishers, 2005) and Brian Steel Will's *A Battle from the Start* (New York: Harper Collins, 1992).

No study of the Ku Klux Klan is complete without an in-depth look at race, prejudice, and violence. For this reading, I turned to George M. Frederickson's *Racism: A Short History* (Princeton, N.J.: Princeton University Press, 2002), Joel Williamson's *A Rage for Order: Black-White Relations in the American South Since Emancipation* (New

York: Oxford University Press, 1986), Elisabeth Young-Breuhl's *The Anatomy of Prejudices* (Cambridge, Mass.: Harvard University Press, 1996); Grace Elizabeth Hale's *Making Whiteness: The Culture of Segregation in the South, 1890–1940* (New York: Vintage Books, 1998); and Marc Aronson's *Race: A History Beyond Black and White* (New York: Simon and Schuster, 2007).

An invaluable resource for understanding prejudice and human behavior is Margot Stern Strom's *Facing History and Ourselves: Holocaust and Human Behavior* (Brookline, Mass.: Facing History and Ourselves National Foundation, Inc., 1994). For alternate viewpoints, I consulted work such as Dinesh D'Souza's *The End of Racism* (New York: Free Press, Simon and Schuster, 1995), in which he argues that a race-obsessed America fails to see the possibility of progress, and Marshall L. DeRosa's *Redeeming American Democracy: Lessons from the Confederate Constitution* (Gretna, La.: Pelican Publishing Company, 2007).

Sociologists and psychologists have long studied the devastating implications of rumor on violence. Excellent resources on this subject include Patricia A. Turner's *I Heard It Through the Grapevine: Rumor in African American Culture* (Berkeley: University of California Press, 1993), *Rumor Mills: The Social Impact of Rumor and Legend* (edited by Gary Fine and others; New Brunswick, N.J.: Aldine Transaction, 2005), and Gordon W. Allport and Leo Postman's *The Psychology of Rumor* (New York: Henry Holt and Company, 1947). This last source is considered a standard on the subject and offers great insight into human behavior.

Today, the Internet is the new grapevine telegraph. For readers who wish to dispel rumors and distinguish facts from fiction, I recommend fact-checking sites such as www.factcheck.org and www.snopes.com. For readers who wish to strengthen their reasoning skills when confronted with rumors, I recommend Nancy M. Cavendar and Howard Kahane's *Logic and Contemporary Rhetoric: The Use of Reason in Everyday Life* (Belmont, Calif.: Wadsworth Publishing, 2009).

Several documentary histories provide an excellent and diverse collection of reprinted primary documents. These include Herbert Aptheker's multivolume *Documentary History of the Negro People of the United States* (Secaucus, N.J.: Citadel Press, 1973) and Walter Fleming's *Documentary History of Reconstruction: Political, Military, Social, Religious, Educational and Industrial, 1865 to the Present Time* (New York: Peter Smith, 1950). Readers should bear in mind that Fleming was among the early-twentieth-century historians who denounced slavery but argued that the freed people were unprepared for citizenship. These historians further argued that victorious Northerners had trampled the rights of white Southerners, who after much suffering banded together to overthrow Republican governments and restore home rule. This interpretation is known as the Dunning School, named after William Archibald Dunning and dominated history textbooks well into the 1960s. Today, historians discredit the racist Dunning school perspective.

I also relied on 1860 and 1870 census records and nineteenth-century newspapers and periodicals. These included *Harper's Weekly, Frank Leslie's Illustrated*

News, Pulaski (Tenn.) Citizen, Cincinnati Commercial, New York Times, American Missionary, Columbia (S.C.) Daily Phoenix, Yorkville (S.C.) Enquirer, Tuskaloosa (Ala.) Independent Monitor, and *Atlantic Monthly,* among others.

Few photographic images of the Reconstruction-era Ku Klux Klan exist. For this reason, *Harper's Weekly* and *Frank Leslie's Illustrated News* were especially valuable for their contemporaneous illustrations. For furthering my understanding on how pictorial newspapers shaped and reflected popular views regarding race, I am grateful for Joshua Brown's *Beyond the Lines: Pictorial Reporting, Everyday Life, and the Crisis of Gilded Age America* (Berkeley: University of California Press, 2002) and his visual essays mentioned earlier.

For the stories of individuals I pored over 8,027 pages of testimony from the Ku Klux Klan trials of 1871–72, collected in thirteen volumes and called *Testimony Taken by the Joint Select Committee to Inquire into the Condition of Affairs in the Late Insurrectionary States,* or the Ku Klux Klan Report. The volumes were published by the Government Printing Offices in Washington in 1872. I also used a sixty-seven-page report of outrages committed in Tennessee and compiled in 1868, called *Report of Evidence Taken Before the Military Committee in Relation to Outrages Committed by the Ku Klux Klan in Middle and West Tennessee.*

Equally valuable were the more than 2,300 Slave Narratives collected by government workers in 1937. The narratives are easily located in the digitized American Memory collection at the Library of Congress website, www.loc.gov. Although some historians question the reliability of these narratives, I found it exciting to compare the particulars of the Slave Narratives against the testimony of the Ku Klux Klan Report. For an absorbing study of slavery and memory, see the works of David W. Blight, Gladys-Marie Fry, and Patricia Turner, as mentioned earlier.

Quotes from the above KKK Report and Slave Narratives are attributed in the section of this book titled "Quote Attributions," as are other primary sources consulted, such as letters, diaries, newspapers, and other accounts.

In addition to reading about the William Luke murder in the Alabama KKK report (as cited in "Quote Attributions"), interested readers can refer to Gene L. Howard's *Death at Cross Plains: An Alabama Reconstruction Tragedy* (Tuscaloosa: University of Alabama Press, 1984) and Peter Meyler's "Strange Fruit. The Martyrdom of William Luke" (*Beaver,* February/March 2005, vol. 85, no. 1, pp. 22–25).

John Fabian DeWitt's *Patriots and Cosmopolitans: Hidden Histories of American Law* offers additional insight into the life of South Carolina freedman Elias Hill, his quest for black citizenship in the United States, and ultimately his decision to leave America for Liberia.

In the midst of researching this book, I attended a Klan Congress (they no longer call it a rally) held deep in Arkansas's Ozark Mountains. I wanted to understand how the present-day Klan read against the Reconstruction era order.

On a dirt road, with my directions unfolded in my lap, I wound my rental car over railroad tracks, over two low-water concrete slabs, through a creek that had overrun its banks, past a trailer with a large

Kerry-Edwards presidential campaign sign (now two years post-election), and past a dilapidated house soldiered by a hundred goats or more.

At a gate marked by a large American flag, I turned in to the Soldiers of the Cross Bible Camp. My car spit dirt and gravel as I continued up the long, steep drive. At the top of the hill, the drive opened onto a clearing lined by red, white, and black flags so similar in color and design to the Nazi swastika that I sucked in my breath.

I parked next to trucks and minivans that sprouted American and Confederate flags from their antennas and headed up the hillside to the community center, where families were milling about. For those readers who wonder if I traveled alone, I did. But my worried husband flew down that night.

There began my weekend with the Klan, a weekend lit with fire-and-brimstone speeches that warned of the dangers of racial integration and Jews; that claimed America; was intended for white people; that condemned public schools and taxes; that burned with an altar call of Klan members, one by one or in family groups, stretching out a right arm in a straight-armed salute, dedicating themselves to their race, their God, and their country and then shouting "white power!" The weekend ended with a twenty-five-foot cross burning against the night sky, surrounded by men and at least two women in white robes.

I had researched the Klan's history and creed, and yet no reading had prepared me for the speakers and the men and older boys who wrapped the tall cross in burlap and the children who donned child-size Klan robes for the closing cross lighting. I

also wasn't prepared for the ordinariness of these people: if I had met them at another time, in another place, if I didn't know their beliefs and their politics, I could see myself swapping recipes and stories about our children. I also wasn't prepared for the relatively small number in attendance— fewer than a hundred—even though the registration packet and other information promised hundreds.

Of all the speeches I heard that weekend, one haunts me more than the others. "We are planting thousands of seeds among high school students," said a Klanswoman who had traveled from Kentucky. "We don't need robes . . . a silent majority in America agrees with us."

My reaction was visceral. That night, I couldn't get the shower hot enough to scrub away the words. I thought about silence and the many ways it implies agreement, whether it's a failure to speak out against a racist or hateful remark or joke or a failure to confront bullying, stereotyping, and scapegoating and other injustices. I also thought about fear, how fear is peddled and how we're often manipulated to fear the wrong things.

The use of terror—the use of violence and fear as a physical and psychological weapon—is as old as humanity. So is silence. It is my hope that this book will show that the lives of the Klan's victims —the lives of people like Anne Evans, Hannah Tutson, Henry Lipscomb, Elias Hill, and William Luke and others— are far greater than the humiliation and violence they suffered at the hands of the Klan. It is my hope that this book will stand in memorial to the victims' great courage and to the pivotal role each one played in American history.

The Southern Poverty Law Center estimates that somewhere across America each week a cross is burned. Some people argue that cross-burning is a symbolic form of speech, protected by the First Amendment. The law, however, allows a court to presume that cross-burning is a threat.

Photograph by the author

ACKNOWLEDGMENTS

For readers interested in more information on tolerance and justice, a good place to start is the Internet. You will find resources such as the Southern Poverty Law Center (SPLC), located in Montgomery, Alabama, and its electronic *Teaching Tolerance* newsletter. (Educators can subscribe free.) The newsletter offers tips to parents, teachers, teenagers, and younger people for everyday action, topics ranging from responding to bigoted comments to dealing with hate at school. The Facing History and Ourselves organization helps educators connect history to current issues in our world today. Committed to developing literacy, the organization offers educator resources and development programs.

My thanks must begin with my gratitude to my history-teaching husband, Joe, for his unwavering support and encouragement in the writing of this book and for his expertise in the areas of U.S. history and political science; to my daughter, Brandy, and her husband, Rick, for the good care they give me while I am on deadline; and to my son, Joe, whose interests and conversations inform my work in a myriad of ways. I also thank my friends Jeanne and Dale McCloe, for their support and for many conversations that have helped to inform this book and Bambi Lobdell and Libby Tucker for their generous assistance with hard-to-get library materials.

To my editor, Ann Rider, and to my publisher, I owe a debt of gratitude for believing in this book. For reading chapters and parts of chapters in early draft form, I thank fellow writers and friends Suzanne Fisher Staples, Gail Carson Levine, Lisa Rowe Fraustino, Clara Gillow Clark, Laura Lee Wren, and Elaine Lisandrelli.

To my gaffe-protection force, I extend a very special thank-you. These include my husband Joe; Dr. Lawrence Kennedy, professor of U.S. history with an emphasis in Reconstruction history, urban studies, and race and ethnic studies at the University of Scranton (Pennsylvania); middle school librarian extraordinaire Janice Borland, sixth grade teacher Becky Brown, and retired eighth-grade English teacher Esther Smith at the Garland Independent School District (Garland, Texas). All mistakes are my own.

I thank the following individuals and institutions for their help in obtaining images, documents, and other important resources: Joshua Brown (American Social History Project, City University of New York); the South Carolina Historical Society; the New York Historical Society; the Beck Center Civil War Site at Emory College; Tim Turner, Tourism Coordinator, Giles County Tourism Foundation (Tennessee); George Newman, Giles County Historical Society (Tennessee); Robert Pickett (Vicksburg, Mississippi); Mark Putuck, Southern Poverty Law Center (Montgomery, Alabama); the amazing reference librarians in the Prints and Photographs Division at the Library of Congress; the reference librarians at the National Archives; and Roxanne Loney at the Scranton Public Library.

Susan Campbell Bartoletti
June 2009

INDEX